Pearson Revise

Pearson Edexcel GCSE (9–1)

German

Second Edition

Revision Workbook

Series Consultant: Harry Smith

Author: Harriette Lanzer

Also available to support your revision:

Revise GCSE Study Skills Guide   9781292318875

The **Revise GCSE Study Skills Guide** is full of tried-and-trusted hints and tips for how to learn more effectively. It gives you techniques to help you achieve your best – throughout your GCSE studies and beyond!

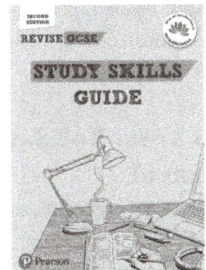

Revise GCSE Revision Planner   9781292318868

The **Revise GCSE Revision Planner** helps you to plan and organise your time, step-by-step, throughout your GCSE revision. Use this book and wall chart to mastermind your revision.

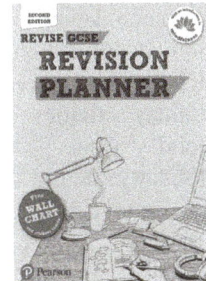

Difficulty scale

The scale next to each exam-style question tells you how difficult it is.

Some questions cover a range of difficulties.

The more of the scale that is shaded, the harder the question is.

Some questions are Foundation level.

Some questions are Higher level.

Some questions are applicable to both levels.

For the full range of Pearson revision titles across KS2, 11+, KS3, GCSE, Functional Skills, AS/A Level and BTEC visit: www.pearsonschools.co.uk/revise

Contents

AUDIO
Audio files for the listening exercises in this book can be accessed by using the QR codes or hotlinks throughout the book, or going to www.pearsonschools.co.uk/mflrevisionaudio

Listen to the recording

A small bit of small print
Pearson Edexcel publishes Sample Assessment Material and the Specification on its website. This is the official content and this book should be used in conjunction with it. The questions in this Workbook have been written to help you practise every topic in the book. Remember: the real exam questions may not look like this.

Physical descriptions

Personal profiles

1 Read the personal profiles on a dating website.

● ● ●	
EYMEN H.	Ich bin größer als meine Freunde und auch sehr schlank. Ich habe braune, glatte Haare – sie sehen oft ein bisschen wild aus!
NILS D.	Meine Augen sind grün und ich trage immer eine Brille. Ich habe einen langen Bart.
ROBERT W.	Ich trage gern einen großen Ohrring im linken Ohr, weil ich das cool finde, aber ich habe keinen Schnurrbart – ich finde das hässlich!
TAIJI F.	Ich habe eine Glatze, also muss ich nie zum Friseur gehen. Ich bin froh darüber!

Don't be confused by a comparative such as *größer* from *groß*, just because it has an umlaut.

What do they say about themselves? Enter either **Eymen**, **Nils**, **Robert** or **Taiji**.

You can use each person more than once.

(a) ....Robert.......... is not keen on facial hair. ✓   **(1 mark)**

(b) ....Nils.......... does not have perfect eyesight. ✓   **(1 mark)**

(c) ....Robert eymen.......... often looks untidy. ✓   **(1 mark)**

(d) ....taiji.......... does not have any hair. ✓   **(1 mark)**

(e) ....Niles.......... has facial hair. ✓   **(1 mark)**

(f) ....robert.......... wears jewellery. ✓   **(1 mark)**

6

Missing child

2 How does Frau Richter describe her missing child at the police station?

Listen to the recording and put a cross [×] in each one of the **three** correct boxes.

Listen to the recording

A	Annabell has short hair.	☒
B	She has curly hair.	☐
C	She is wearing a T-shirt.	☐
D	She is average height.	☒
E	She is not very tall.	☐
F	She occasionally wears an earring.	☒
G	She sometimes needs help to see.	☐

(3 marks)

Character descriptions

Family descriptions

1 Read Sura's blog.

> Kadir ist fünfzehn Jahre alt und wir verstehen uns seit der Kindheit wirklich sehr gut, weil wir viele Interessen gemeinsam haben. Als Kadir sehr klein war, war er schüchtern und ziemlich ernst. Wenn ein Erwachsener ihm eine Frage stellte, musste ich als seine ältere Schwester die Antwort darauf geben.
>
> Ich bin zwar ein bisschen faul, aber Kadir ist das nie, weil er zu viel Energie hat, um bloß auf dem Sofa zu sitzen! In der Schule ist er besonders fleißig und er hat nie Probleme mit den Hausaufgaben, obwohl ich finde, dass er zu oft Informationen direkt vom Internet abschreibt.

Read the text first of all for the gist. Then read it again, keeping an eye on the statements you have to choose from.

What is the blog about? Put a cross [x] in each one of the **three** correct boxes.

A	Sura and Kadir have never had anything in common.	☐
B	Kadir likes many of the activities Sura enjoys.	☐
C	Kadir used to be more confident than Sura.	☐
D	Sura used to ask adults lots of questions.	☐
E	Kadir interacts better with adults now.	☐
F	Kadir often lazes about at home.	☐
G	Kadir keeps up-to-date with his school work.	☐

(3 marks)

The neighbours

2 Gabi is describing her neighbours. What does she say?

Listen to the recording and complete the sentences by putting a cross [x] in the correct box for each question.

Listen to the recording

(i) Yesterday Gabi noted her neigbours' …

☐	A impatience
☐	B sense of humour
☐	C loudness
☐	D generosity

(1 mark)

(ii) The father was …

☐	A lazy
☐	B hard-working
☐	C clever
☐	D bored

(1 mark)

(iii) The children behaved …

☐	A well
☐	B badly
☐	C rudely
☐	D normally

(1 mark)

Family

Meine Familie

1   Lies diesen Blog von Till.

> ● ● ●
>
> Als ich in der Grundschule war, haben wir in Wien gewohnt. In derselben Stadt waren meine Großeltern und meine Tanten, und ich habe einmal pro Woche mit meinen zwei Cousinen gespielt.
>
> Weil meine Eltern oft bis zehn Uhr abends arbeiten mussten, hat meine Tante Julia nach der Schule auf mich aufgepasst. Meine Tante ist ebenso streng wie Mutti und Vati, und ich musste immer Hausaufgaben machen, bevor ich spielen oder fernsehen durfte.
>
> Vor vier Jahren mussten wir nach Salzburg ziehen, weil meine Eltern sich dort erfolgreich auf Stellen bei einer großen Firma beworben haben. Ich war sehr traurig, dass ich meine Umgebung sowie meine Cousinen verlassen musste und jetzt weit von ihnen entfernt wohne.

Wähl die richtige Antwort [×].

(i) Als Kind wohnten … in der Nähe.

☐	**A** Tills Freunde
☐	**B** Tills Verwandte
☐	**C** keine Familienmitglieder
☐	**D** keine Cousinen

(1 mark)

(ii) Till hat … Zeit mit seinen Cousinen verbracht.

☐	**A** regelmäßig
☐	**B** nie
☐	**C** selten
☐	**D** kaum

(1 mark)

(iii) Tills Eltern haben bis … gearbeitet.

☐	**A** zum Abendessen
☐	**B** vier Uhr
☐	**C** Mittag
☐	**D** spät

(1 mark)

(iv) Tante Julia war … Tills Eltern.

☐	**A** lockerer als
☐	**B** nicht so autoritär wie
☐	**C** genauso streng wie
☐	**D** strenger als

(1 mark)

(v) Till war …, dass er umziehen musste.

☐	**A** froh
☐	**B** überrascht
☐	**C** es egal
☐	**D** unglücklich

(1 mark)

Familien in Not

2   You hear a radio interview with Frau Hartfiel from a charity working with families in need. What does she say? Choose the **two** correct answers.

> Read the answer choices before you listen to the recording – only two match the recording. Highlight key words and think about what they are in German. Can you hear any of them as you listen?

Listen to the recording

A	The current situation is not what people would expect of Austria.	☐
B	The situation is exactly the same across the whole country.	☐
C	The charity is asking for donations of money.	☐
D	Young parents are sometimes not aware of the importance of breakfast.	☐
E	Most children have breakfast before school.	☐

(2 marks)

Friends

Meine Freunde

1 Übersetze **ins Deutsche**.

> Revise possessive pronouns, such as *mein*, *dein* and *unser* and their endings – look at page 88 in the Grammar section to check.

(a) I love my friends.

Ich liebe .... **(2 marks)**

(b) My friend Lotti is very nice.

Meine ....

.... **(2 marks)**

(c) She lives next to the station in Berlin.

....

.... **(2 marks)**

(d) Last week we went to the cinema together.

....

.... **(3 marks)**

(e) We laughed a lot, because we watched a funny film.

....

.... **(3 marks)**

Meine Freunde

2 Übersetze **ins Deutsche**.

> There are 12 marks for this task and four sentences to be translated, which become progressively more difficult. Share the time available to make sure you cover each sentence.

> Yesterday I visited my friend Yusuf to play computer games. His brother is very annoying. Yusuf often comes to my house but I want him to come on his own. I prefer to spend time with Yusuf as we get on really well.

Gestern ....

....

....

....

....

....

....

....

.... **(12 marks)**

Role models

The singer Hoth

1   Read this blog post by the singer, Hoth.

> ● ● ●
>
> Ich bin seit zwei Jahren berühmt. Ich bin Sänger, und die jüngere Generation liebt meine Lieder besonders. Ich habe viele Fans in der ganzen Welt, und sie schicken mir oft Briefe und Geschenke.
>
> Als Vorbild versuche ich immer, meinen Fans persönlich zu danken. Am Wochenende sitze ich in meinem Arbeitszimmer und spreche per Internet mit ihnen. Ich will kein egoistischer Star sein.

Complete the gap in each sentence using a word from the box below. There are more words than gaps.

> There are two words which could grammatically fit each gap – work out what they are and then select the correct one to match the text.

> | pictures | study | badly | musical | many |
> |---|---|---|---|---|
> | kitchen | well | sporty | few | gifts | student |

(a)   Hoth is ....   **(1 mark)**

(b)   Hoth's fans live in .... countries.   **(1 mark)**

(c)   Hoth's fans send him ....   **(1 mark)**

(d)   Hoth spends the weekend in his ....   **(1 mark)**

(e)   Hoth treats his fans ....   **(1 mark)**

German celebrities

LISTENING TRACK 4

Listen to the recording

2   You hear a report on German radio about role models.

What does the report say about role models?

Listen to the recording and put a cross [×] in each one of the **three** correct boxes.

A	German celebrities successfully hide their private lives.	☐
B	German celebrities are unhappy about being in the news.	☐
C	Role models are unnecessary.	☐
D	Most people enjoy comparing their lives to a role model's life.	☐
E	Role models make people feel bad about themselves.	☐
F	Role models don't change people's lives.	☐
G	It is not a good idea to rely on role models too much.	☐

> For the Higher listening passages, you will need to know your tenses: make sure you revise them thoroughly before the exams.

(3 marks)

Relationships

Translation

Guided

1   Translate this passage **into English**.

> Mein Bruder geht mir auf die Nerven. Abends hört er Musik. Das ist schlecht, weil ich lieber Klavier übe. Gestern bin ich mit meinen Freundinnen ins Konzert gegangen.
> Am Wochenende bleiben wir zu Hause.

My ....

In the evenings ....

That is ....

Yesterday ....

....

....

> The past participle is at the end of the sentence – check on page 100 in the Grammar section to make sure you are confident with the perfect tense.

At ....

> Check tenses carefully.

....

.... **(7 marks)**

Luke's sister

LISTENING TRACK 5

Listen to the recording

2   You hear this podcast on the radio.

What do you find out about Luke's sister?

Listen to the recording and complete the sentences by putting a cross [×] in the correct box for each question.

(i)   Luke puts their problem down to their …

☐	**A** tastes in music
☐	**B** ages
☐	**C** shared hobbies
☐	**D** toys

(1 mark)

(ii)   They have to …

☐	**A** do the same hobbies
☐	**B** play together
☐	**C** watch TV in their rooms
☐	**D** share the TV

(1 mark)

(iii) Luke finds his sister …

☐	**A** mature
☐	**B** mean
☐	**C** funny
☐	**D** clever

(1 mark)

When I was younger

The Conversation is the final section in the Speaking exam. It should last about 5–6 minutes (Parts 1 and 2) and cover two topics, one of which you will have chosen in advance.

Matching questions and answers

1   Match the student's replies (A–D) to the teacher's questions (1–4). Draw lines to link them.

Have a good supply of idioms and expressions which you can transfer to any topic, such as *meiner Meinung nach* and *es ist schade, dass …*

1   Woran erinnerst du dich am meisten aus deiner Kindheit?

A   Mit fünf Jahren ist man meiner Meinung nach viel zu jung, um in die Schule zu gehen. In Deutschland ist es besser, weil man erst mit sieben Jahren in die Schule muss. Es ist schade, dass wir das hier in England nicht machen.

2   Was hast du gern in der Grundschule gemacht?

B   Ich erinnere mich besonders an den Kindergarten, denn wir haben den ganzen Tag nur gebastelt und gespielt. Das hat echt viel Spaß gemacht.

3   In welchem Alter sollte man mit der Schule anfangen?

C   In der Grundschule war ich ziemlich schüchtern und ich habe oft alleine auf dem Pausenhof gespielt. Ich habe die Fächer nicht so interessant gefunden, aber die Grundschullehrer waren sehr sympathisch.

4   Wie werden Kinder in der Zukunft anders leben?

D   Kinder werden in ein paar Jahren genauso sein wie jetzt. Sie werden immer noch mit Puppen und Fußbällen spielen und sie werden immer noch weinen und lachen. Bestimmt werden sie öfter am Bildschirm sitzen und daher werden sie nicht sehr gesund sein.

2   Listen to the student's answers, paying particular attention to the pronunciation of words with umlauts such as *Fächer*, *fünf* and *öfter*.

Listen to the recording

Peer group

Die Freundesgruppe

1 Look at the photo and read the task.

Du bist im Skatepark mit deinen Freunden. Du postest dieses Foto online.

Beschreib das Foto **und** schreib deine Meinung über Freundesgruppen.

Schreib ungefähr 20–30 Wörter **auf Deutsch**.

Now choose the best student response to the task. Justify your choice.

> The verb in a German sentence comes in second position: *Man **sieht** …* or *Im Bild **sieht** man …*

(a) Ich bin mit meinen Freunden im Skateboardpark. Wir treffen uns hier, um Skateboard zu fahren. Ich trage ein T-Shirt und eine Jeans.

(b) Ich fahre mit Freunden Skateboard im Park. Das finde ich super, weil meine Freunde mir sehr wichtig sind. Ich bin immer froh, wenn wir zusammen etwas unternehmen.

(c) Ich bin mit meinen Freunden im Park. Meine Freunde sind mir wichtig.

(d) Ich bin mit einer Gruppe von Freunden im Skatepark. Wir treffen uns jeden Mittwoch nach der Schule an diesem Ort, weil wir alle in der Nähe wohnen. Meine Freunde sind mir am wichtigsten und wir machen immer neue Pläne, um uns echt gut zu unterhalten.

(e) Wir sind im Park. Ich mag meine Gruppe von Freunden sehr, weil wir dieselben Interessen haben. Zum Beispiel fahren wir alle gern Skateboard und wir gehen auch gern ins Kino. Es macht immer Spaß mit Freunden, denke ich.

My choice is ( ) because ....

....

....

My photo message

2 Now complete the task above for yourself, using the student's 'perfect answer' to help you.

> Keep an eye on your word count. Make sure you cover both parts of the question: photo description **and** the opinion asked for.

....

....

.... **(12 marks)**

Customs

How does Switzerland compare?

1   Read this competition entry for a Swiss language website.

> **Das Leben in der Schweiz**
>
> In der Schweiz ist das Leben anders als in England. Wir fahren auf der rechten Seite – in England fährt man links. Hier muss man entweder „du" oder „Sie" benutzen, weil das höflich ist. In Großbritannien habt ihr nur ein Wort dafür!
>
> Wenn man in der Schweiz nicht alles versteht, kann man fragen: „Könnten Sie bitte langsamer sprechen?" Die Leute reden oft zu schnell!

Complete the gap in each sentence using a word from the box below.
There are more words than gaps.

> | polite | explain | he | slowly | left | right |
> |---|---|---|---|---|---|
> | you | understand | fast | friendly | people | |

(a) The writer drives on the ....   **(1 mark)**

(b) To be .... you should choose the correct form of address.   **(1 mark)**

(c) There is one word for .... in English.   **(1 mark)**

(d) Some people have trouble to ....   **(1 mark)**

(e) People often speak ....   **(1 mark)**

Different ways of life

2   You hear this interview with a Chinese visitor about her impressions of Europe.

> You will hear the recording twice, so make notes the first time round and then decide on your final answer on the second listening.

Listen to the recording and answer the following questions **in English**. You do not need to write in full sentences.

Listen to the recording

(a) What made the biggest impression on this visitor?

....   **(1 mark)**

(b) Where did the visitor experience the difference in problem-solving skills?

....   **(1 mark)**

(c) What reason does she give for the German approach?

....   **(1 mark)**

(d) What does the visitor recommend for people who want to visit China?
     Give **two** details.

....

....   **(2 marks)**

Home

Die neuen Leiden des jungen W. **by Ulrich Plenzdorf**

> Even though this is a literary extract, treat it as any other reading passage. Use the strategies you have developed to help you understand it.

> Literary extracts often rely on the imperfect tense (see page 102 in the Grammar section) for telling their story, so make sure you can recognise key forms, such as *saß* from *sitzen*, *fiel* from *fallen* and *verstand* from *verstehen*.

1 Read the extract from the text.

Edgar, the narrator who is in love with Dieter's fiancée Charlie (Charlotte), is visiting Dieter's room, and needs to make up an excuse for what he is doing there.

> Jedenfalls holte sie mich ins Zimmer. Im Zimmer saß Dieter. Er hatte den Schreibtisch am Fenster stehen und saß davor, mit dem Rücken zum Zimmer. Ich verstand das völlig. Wenn einer nur ein Zimmer hat, in dem er auch arbeiten muss, dann muss er sich irgendwie abschirmen. Sein Rücken war praktisch eine Wand.
>
> Charlotte sagte: Dreh dich mal um!
>
> Dieter drehte sich um, und mir fiel zum Glück ein: Wollte nur fragen, ob ihr nicht 'nen Schraubenschlüssel* habt.
>
> Ich wurde einfach das Gefühl nicht los, Dieter sollte vielleicht gar nicht wissen, dass Charlie mich eingeladen hatte.
>
> Komischerweise sagte Charlie: Haben wir einen Schraubenschlüssel?

> Use your vocabulary knowledge to help you with unfamiliar words. For example, you know a *Rucksack* is a 'rucksack' (a bag carried on the back); you probably know *zurückkommen* means 'to come back', so what do you think a *Rücken* is?

* **Schraubenschlüssel** = *spanner*

> Watch out for the pluperfect tense: *eingeladen hatte* (had invited) is not the same as *eingeladen hat* (invited).

Answer the following questions **in English**. You do not need to write in full sentences.

(a) What was unusual in how Dieter was sitting?

.... **(1 mark)**

(b) Why had Dieter arranged his room as he did?

.... **(1 mark)**

(c) How did Dieter create a barrier?

.... **(1 mark)**

(d) Where was Charlotte in relation to Dieter?

.... **(1 mark)**

(e) What did the narrator not want Dieter to know?

.... **(1 mark)**

10

Everyday life

Daily routine

1 Luisa is interviewed about her daily routine.

Listen to the interview and complete the sentences by putting a cross [×] in the correct box for each question.

Listen to the recording

> Listen to the recording first to get the gist of the passage; then concentrate on the multiple choice options and see how many you can identify, and also if there are any you can discount straight away.

> This task is split into two parts, each with its own recording – use the parts to help orientate yourself and keep up with the recording; it will not stop when you want it to!

Part (a)

(i) Luisa sees her family …

☐	**A** at breakfast
☐	**B** rarely
☐	**C** after breakfast
☐	**D** in the bathroom

(1 mark)

(ii) Luisa is sometimes delayed by …

☐	**A** getting petrol
☐	**B** busy roads
☐	**C** twenty minutes
☐	**D** roadworks

(1 mark)

(iii) Luisa knows she should …

☐	**A** buy more petrol
☐	**B** share her car
☐	**C** not use the air conditioning
☐	**D** change her form of travel

(1 mark)

> You might hear all the answer options for question (ii) in the recording, but it is the one thing which causes a delay which is key here.

The interview continues.

Part (b)

Listen to the recording

> Make sure you don't switch off as soon as Part (a) is complete – you are only halfway through the task.

(i) Luisa … late for work.

☐	**A** is sometimes
☐	**B** would like to be
☐	**C** is not concerned about being
☐	**D** has never been

(1 mark)

(ii) Luisa's work days are …

☐	**A** full of variety
☐	**B** unpredictable
☐	**C** the same
☐	**D** interesting

(1 mark)

(iii) Luisa … her drinks break.

☐	**A** enjoys
☐	**B** doesn't always have
☐	**C** is alone for
☐	**D** misses

(1 mark)

> During your second listening, make sure you do not leave any answers blank – you will not hear the recording again, so you must be definite with your decision-making here.

LISTENING TRACK 8a

LISTENING TRACK 8b

Meals at home

Die verlorene Ehre der Katharina Blum by Heinrich Böll

1 Read the extract from the text.

It is breakfast time at Trude's house.

> Trude hatte schon die Kaffeemaschine angemacht und wusch sich im Bad. Die Zeitung lag im Salon auf dem Tisch und zwei Telegramme.
>
> Es war gerade acht Uhr fünfzehn und fast genau die Zeit, zu der ihnen sonst Katharina das Frühstück servierte: hübsch wie sie immer den Tisch deckte, mit Blumen und frisch gewaschenen Tüchern und Servietten, vielerlei Brot und Honig, Eiern und Kaffee und für Trude Toast und Orangenmarmelade.
>
> Sogar Trude war sentimental, als sie die Kaffeemaschine, ein bisschen Knäckebrot, Honig und Butter brachte.
>
> »Es wird nie mehr so sein, nie mehr.«

Answer the following questions **in English**. You do not have to write in full sentences.

(a) What had Trude done before taking a bath?

.... **(1 mark)**

(b) What time was breakfast normally?

.... **(1 mark)**

(c) Name **one** item, other than food, that Katharina usually put on the table.

.... **(1 mark)**

(d) Name **one** food item which was only for Trude.

.... **(1 mark)**

(e) Why did Trude feel wistful?

.... **(1 mark)**

Mealtimes

2 Your exchange partner, Christian, is telling you about mealtimes at his house.

> You are listening for what Christian **likes**, so pay attention to opinion words here.

Listen to the recording

What does Christian enjoy about mealtimes?

Listen to the recording and put a cross [×] in each one of the **three** correct boxes.

A	meat	☐
B	vegetables	☐
C	salt	☐
D	evening meal	☐
E	eating with parents	☐
F	eating at table	☐
G	breakfast	☐

(3 marks)

Food and drink

Celebrity chef at home

1   Read the magazine extract about the celebrity chef.

> „Es schmeckt total anders, wenn ich hier zu Hause koche, als wenn ich unter der Studiobeleuchtung Lammfleisch mit Soße und Bratkartoffeln für die Zuschauer vorbereiten muss", sagt er.
>
> Gestern war ich bei Benedikt Popel. Am Abend vorher hatte er schon einen Pizzateig aus Mehl, Öl, Hefe und Wasser vorbereitet. Bei meiner Ankunft hat er erst begonnen, die anderen Zutaten auf den Teig zu legen: Zwiebeln, Schinken, Käse und Oliven. „Das lieben meine Kinder am meisten", erklärte er lächelnd.
>
> „Mittagessen bei uns ist immer chaotisch", sagt er. „Gestern zum Beispiel gab es wegen der Nachspeise großen Krach! Ich habe eine Obsttorte vorbereitet, aber ich hatte leider vergessen, dass unsere Jüngste keine Ananas mag und ich musste schnell eine Schokoladenmilch mit Eis für sie machen!"

Put a cross [x] in the correct box.

(i)   Food cooked at home is … television food.

☐	**A** better than
☐	**B** the same as
☐	**C** not as attractive as
☐	**D** more expensive than

(1 mark)

(ii) Benedikt prepared the pizza base …

☐	**A** yesterday
☐	**B** the day before yesterday
☐	**C** with the reporter
☐	**D** in the morning

(1 mark)

(iii) Benedikt chose toppings to …

☐	**A** impress the reporter
☐	**B** cheer himself up
☐	**C** surprise his children
☐	**D** please his family

(1 mark)

(iv) Yesterday's lunch was …

☐	**A** disliked by everybody
☐	**B** a complete disaster
☐	**C** problematic
☐	**D** late in arriving

(1 mark)

(v)   Benedikt saved the day by …

☐	**A** buying another dessert
☐	**B** making another tart
☐	**C** removing the pineapple chunks
☐	**D** making an alternative dessert

(1 mark)

Favourite foods

2   Hella and her friends are talking about their favourite foods. What do they say?
    Listen to the recording and put a cross [x] in each one of the **three** correct boxes.

A	I think salad is tasty.	☐
B	I never eat cucumber.	☐
C	I love cauliflower.	☐
D	I don't like vegetables.	☐
E	I eat eggs for breakfast.	☐
F	I enjoy toast for breakfast.	☐
G	I love a fried egg for lunch.	☐

Listen to the recording

Look at the sentences first and remind yourself of the German words for the key food items. Then listen out for them.

(3 marks)

13

Shopping for clothes

Translation

Guided

1 Translate this passage **into English**.

> Kleider einkaufen kann sehr anstrengend sein.
> Man kann im Kaufhaus preiswerte Kleidungsstücke
> finden und auch auf dem Markt. Ich würde allen
> Kunden vorschlagen, die Kleider immer in der
> Umkleidekabine richtig anzuprobieren. Man kann die
> Einkäufe umtauschen, wenn es ein Problem gibt.

> Read the whole extract through once, to get
> an idea of the theme and ideas or message.
> Translate each sentence one by one: the
> first sentence is the most straightforward,
> so leave yourself enough time for the more
> challenging sentences ahead.

Buying ....

....

You can ....

....

....

....

....

....

....

> Look at the end of
> the clause for the
> infinitive to go
> with a modal verb
> such as *können*.

(7 marks)

At the department store

2 Du machst ein Berufspraktikum in einem Kaufhaus in
Wien und hörst dieses Gespräch.

Füll die Lücke in jedem Satz mit einem Wort aus dem
Kasten aus. Es gibt mehr Wörter als Lücken.

> For each gap there are two words here
> which fit grammatically – in sentence (a)
> you are looking for a noun after *ein*, so you
> can narrow your options straight away. Then
> you need to make sure that the noun you
> choose matches the sense of the recording.

Listen to the recording

| Maus | 94 | Größen | bunte | 31. | Sweatshirt |
| 49 | Familienmitglied | dunkle | 21. | Farben |

(a) Das Geschenk ist für ein ....   **(1 mark)**

(b) Das Hemd muss eine .... Farbe haben.   **(1 mark)**

(c) Das Hemd ist für ein Fest am .... des Monats.   **(1 mark)**

(d) Es gibt nicht alle .... bei den schwarzen Hemden.   **(1 mark)**

(e) Die Hemden kosten mindestens .... Euro.   **(1 mark)**

Social media

Swiss teenagers and social media

1 Dr Kullik, an expert in social media, is discussing the topic of social media and teenagers on Swiss radio.

Listen to the discussion and answer the following questions **in English**. You do not need to write in full sentences.

> Underline key words in the questions before you listen, to help you focus on the answers.

Part (a)

(i) Give **one** aspect of social media's effect on young people.

.... **(1 mark)**

(ii) What statistic is given regarding social media use?

.... **(1 mark)**

(iii) Why does the expert think the trend cannot be stopped?

.... **(1 mark)**

(iv) What is the key difference between meeting someone online and in reality?

.... **(1 mark)**

Part (b)

The interview continues with a teenager.

> Watch out – if there are separable verbs in listening extracts, you might not hear the whole verb until the end of the clause.

(i) What does Sebastian view as the biggest advantage of social networks?

.... **(1 mark)**

(ii) How has he managed to be one step ahead of his parents?

.... **(1 mark)**

(iii) Why does he feel this is justified? Give **two** reasons.

....

.... **(2 marks)**

(iv) What will happen if parents interfere too much?

.... **(1 mark)**

Listen to the recording

Listen to the recording

Technology

Die Technologie

1   Lies diesen Chatraumeintrag von Delali.

> ● ● ●
>
> In der Grundschule habe ich mein erstes Handy bekommen. Jetzt in der Sekundarschule habe ich das natürlich gegen das neueste Smartphone ausgewechselt.
>
> Meine Freunde benutzen immer Technologie. Das ist unterhaltsam und wir sind nie einsam.
>
> Es ist heutzutage einfacher, sich die vielen Passwörter zu merken als die Geburtstage der Verwandten. So ist wohl unser vernetztes modernes Leben.
>
> Nicht nur ein Computer gehört dazu, sondern auch eine Netzwerkkamera oder ein digitaler Fotoapparat. Man muss unbedingt jede Einzelheit seines täglichen Lebens mit der Welt teilen. Und zwar sofort.

Wähl die richtige Antwort [x].

(i)   Sie hat zwei … gehabt.

☐	A Ideen
☐	B Fotoapparate
☐	C Computer
☐	D Telefone

(1 mark)

> Just because *unterhaltsam* is in the text and linked to option C in question (ii), does not necessarily mean this is the correct answer. Read around the word to get the context – a link alone is not enough.

(ii)   Technologie sorgt dafür, dass man sich nie …

☐	A langweilt.
☐	B streitet.
☐	C unterhält.
☐	D Sendungen ansieht.

(1 mark)

(iii) Leute heute erinnern sich problemlos an …

☐	A Passwörter.
☐	B ihre Adresse.
☐	C Geburtstage.
☐	D ihre Telefonnummer.

(1 mark)

(iv) Ein Computer allein ist …

☐	A am wichtigsten.
☐	B ideal.
☐	C nicht genug.
☐	D notwendig.

(1 mark)

(v)   Für junge Leute ist es …, Fotos zu teilen.

☐	A langweilig
☐	B wichtig
☐	C ungerecht
☐	D altmodisch

(1 mark)

> Build a word bank for yourself, starting with the adjectives on this page, and add to them as you work through the book – they will stand you in good stead across all four skills in the exams.

Online activities

Topic: Online life

My photo description

1 Look at the picture-based task for the photo and read this student's answers to the first two bullet points. Then prepare your own answers to the remaining three bullet points.

Schau dir das Foto an und sei bereit, über Folgendes zu sprechen:

> This rubric is always the same and means 'Look at the photo and be prepared to speak about the following:'

- **Beschreibung des Fotos**

Das Bild zeigt ein Mädchen, das auf seinem Bett liegt. Sie ist ein Teenager und sie hat lange glatte Haare. Sie trägt Kopfhörer, und sie lächelt, weil sie glücklich ist. Im Vordergrund hat sie einen Computer, aber sie benutzt ihn nicht, weil sie sich auf das Handy konzentriert. Das Mädchen trägt einen hellen kurzen Pullover, und ihr Schlafzimmer sieht schön aus.

> Your first task is to say something factual about the photo, i.e. **describe** what you can see. You could describe where it is set, who is in it, what they are wearing, or anything else you can **see** in the photo.

> This student has used a relative pronoun here (*ein Mädchen, das*) – a useful construction to use when describing a person in a picture.

- **Deine Meinung zu Online-Aktivitäten**

Ich finde Online-Aktivitäten super, weil sie so praktisch sind. Wenn ich Probleme mit den Hausaufgaben habe, suche ich die Informationen sofort im Internet. Es ist auch gut, dass man Kinokarten online kaufen kann, weil das Zeit spart. Schlecht daran ist aber, dass man vielleicht zu viel Zeit am Bildschirm verbringt. Es ist sicher gefährlich, wenn man stundenlang am Computer sitzt.

> Here you need to give your opinion. Words such as *Meinung, meinen, denken, finden* all indicate your teacher is looking for an opinion. You can use the present tense for this.

> The bullet points from now on are about the theme of the photo and no longer about the image itself.

- **Online-Aktivitäten, die du gestern gemacht hast**

> When you discuss something you have done, use the past tense, following the lead from the phrase *die du gestern gemacht hast*.

- **Was du heute Abend online machen willst**

> This next bullet point refers to the future with a modal construction. Make sure you use this in your answer: *Heute Abend will ich … machen.*

- **Ob Technologie unterhaltsam und lustig ist**

> The final bullet point is once again looking for your opinion. Start your opinion with a phrase, such as: *Ich finde, Ich glaube, Meiner Meinung nach ist …*
>
> Try to include constructions such as *wenn* clauses and *entweder … oder* (either … or) to add variety to your opinions.

2 Listen to the first part of the student's answer, prepare your own answers to the remaining three sections, then look at the Answer section on page 122 to read and listen to the student's answers to the task in full.

Listen to the recording

> If you don't say enough in response to a bullet point, your teacher may prompt you with further questions, such as: *Warum? Warum nicht? Noch etwas?*

> Practise your pronunciation – listen to the first response and repeat it after the speaker. Record yourself so you can listen to how 'German' you sound. Key sounds to get right here include: *Mädchen, glücklich, Vordergrund, weil* and *sich.*

For and against technology

READING

Guided

Translation

1 Translate this passage **into English**.

> Das Internet macht Spaß, aber es ist auch gefährlich. Der größte Vorteil für mich ist, dass ich mit Verwandten überall in der Welt in Kontakt bleiben kann. Ich mache aber keine Einkäufe online. Letztes Jahr hat jemand meine persönlichen Daten gestohlen und das ist ein Risiko des virtuellen Lebens.

The internet ....

The biggest ....

....

....

But I don't ....

> Use common sense and context to help you understand unfamiliar words: if you don't know who *Verwandten* are, think about what sort of people you might want to stay in contact with.

....

....

....

....

....

....

....

....

....   **(7 marks)**

LISTENING
TRACK 14

Listen to the recording

Technology pros and cons

2 Your German teacher is talking about her pupils and technology.

What does she say about them?

Listen to the recording and put a cross [×] in each one of the **three** correct boxes.

A	finds technology sociable	☐
B	dislikes meeting people	☐
C	finds technology exciting	☐
D	finds equipment frustrating	☐
E	finds games important	☐
F	has a fixed computer	☐
G	finds technology expensive	☐

(3 marks)

Hobbies

Website profile

1 Read Marven's extract from his profile page.

> ● ● ●
>
> Ich bin musikalisch und spiele gern Klavier. Ich übe dreimal pro Woche und am Samstagnachmittag habe ich eine Stunde Unterricht.
>
> Ich lerne auch Schlagzeug, aber das spiele ich nicht im Schlafzimmer. Das muss ich in der Garage spielen.
>
> Ich höre auch gern Musik. Früher habe ich gern Popmusik und Volksmusik gehört, aber jetzt finde ich das total schrecklich. Rockmusik und Tanzmusik finde ich besonders toll, und auch klassische Musik.

Answer the following questions **in English**. You do not need to write in full sentences.

(a) What instrument does Marven practise three times a week?

.... **(1 mark)**

(b) Where does he play the drums?

.... in the garage .... **(1 mark)**

(c) Give **two** types of music Marven likes listening to.

.... rock music & classical music ....

.... **(2 marks)**

> Watch out for question (c)! You need types of music Marven **likes** listening to, not just types of music he mentions.

Hobbys

2 Du hörst einen Bericht im Schulradio über Hobbys.

Wie sind die Hobbys? Trag entweder **toll**, **langweilig**, **anstrengend** oder **gefährlich** ein. Du kannst jedes Wort mehr als einmal verwenden.

> Check you know what these four key adjectives mean before you listen.

Listen to the recording

(a) Skifahren ist .... **(1 mark)**

(b) Schwimmen ist .... **(1 mark)**

(c) Fernsehen ist .... **(1 mark)**

(d) Computer sind manchmal .... **(1 mark)**

(e) Draußen trainieren ist .... **(1 mark)**

Interests

Jugendinteressen

1 Lies diesen Artikel über You-Besuch, einen Treffpunkt zum Thema Jugendhobbys.

● ● ●

Was macht die heutige Jugend wirklich lieber in ihrer Freizeit? Diese Frage haben wir den Besuchern und Besucherinnen der Freizeit-Ausstellung „You-Besuch" gestellt. Die Messe ist von Freitag bis Sonntag von 10 bis 18 Uhr geöffnet.

Viele Besucher möchten in Zukunft ihr Hobby zum Beruf machen.

Nathalie ist am Gymnasium und sie langweilt sich nach der Schule nie. „Ich treffe mich gern mit Freundinnen, mache lange Anrufe und gehe gern einkaufen", erzählte sie uns. „Die Freizeit macht mir großes Vergnügen. Es ist schade, wenn man keine Freude in der Freizeit hat."

Peggy ist zum vierten Mal auf der Jugendmesse. „Hier kann man viel zum Thema Freizeit mitnehmen!" In ihrer Tasche hat sie Getränke, Kugelschreiber, Broschüren und nützliche Adressen.

Beantworte die Fragen **auf Deutsch**. Vollständige Sätze sind nicht nötig.

> Any answers you write here in English will not count, so you must use German words to express your answers. Just write key words – but remember it is unlikely that you will be able to copy the correct answer straight from the text.

(a) Worum geht es bei You-Besuch?

.... **(1 mark)**

(b) Wie viele Tage läuft die Ausstellung?

.... **(1 mark)**

(c) Wie kann ein Hobby später auch nützlich sein?

.... **(1 mark)**

(d) Was ist Nathalies Meinung zum Thema Freizeit?

.... **(1 mark)**

(e) Was findet Peggy besonders nützlich an der Ausstellung?

.... **(1 mark)**

> Make sure you learn the German question words for dealing with tasks like this one.

Music

Peter and music

1 Peter is interviewed about his interest in music.

Listen to the interview and put a cross [×] in the correct box for each question.

Part (a)

(i) It is Peter's dream to …

	A	improve at the flute
☐	B	play the flute in the orchestra
☐	C	learn a new instrument
☐	D	play in the school orchestra

(1 mark)

(ii) Peter is … that he can't have more music lessons.

☐	A	happy
☐	B	not bothered
☐	C	surprised
☐	D	disappointed

(1 mark)

(iii) Peter won't be able to listen to music before …

☐	A	he receives a present
☐	B	the summer
☐	C	he finds his MP3 player
☐	D	he buys himself an MP3 player

(1 mark)

> You won't hear any of these adjectives spelled out to you – you need to understand the gist of what Peter says about music lessons.

The interview continues.

Part (b)

(i) Peter goes to concerts …

☐	A	every weekend
☐	B	occasionally
☐	C	on Sunday evenings
☐	D	rarely

(1 mark)

> Watch out for 'false friends' in listening passages, such as *Sonnabend* – what day of the week is this?

(ii) On the night of the concert, Peter …

☐	A	had to change his plans
☐	B	heard lots of great songs
☐	C	met the lead singer
☐	D	was ill

(1 mark)

(iii) Peter … playing live.

☐	A	dislikes
☐	B	is bored with
☐	C	loves
☐	D	has no experience of

(1 mark)

> Listen for a synonym here – and think about what *stehen auf* might mean.

21

Had a go ☐   **Nearly there** ☐   **Nailed it!** ☐

Sport

Sportfest

1 Read the extended writing task and one student's answers covering the first two bullet points.

> You will have a choice of two tasks on the exam paper, so read them both carefully, and decide which topic area you feel more confident with. Then stick with that choice!

Du organisierst ein Sportfest.

Schreib einen Brief an die Schülerzeitung über das Event.

> The introduction sets the scene and tells you what you are writing.

Du **musst** über diese Punkte schreiben:

> This tells you that you have to include the following points.

- **Details des Events**
Nächste Woche werden wir wieder ein Sportfest für die neunte Klasse veranstalten. Das Fest ist kostenlos, aber man muss einen Platz online reservieren. Wir wollen Interesse an neuen Sportarten bei euch wecken.

> The first point is a gentle start – present tense, and an opportunity to choose details which will show off vocabulary you know about that topic.

- **warum das Event letztes Jahr beliebt war**
Letztes Jahr war dieses Event sehr beliebt, weil das Fest die ideale Gelegenheit war, aufregende Sportarten auszuprobieren. Die Trainer waren wie immer freundlich und sie haben alle Fragen beantwortet.

> This needs the past tense and a justification: why did people come to the event in the past?

- **die Vorteile der angebotenen Sportarten**

> This asks for advantages. Make sure you have lots of positive adjectives to explain your ideas.

- **Pläne für die Zukunft.**

> The word *Zukunft* (future) means you will need to use the future tense and/or the conditional.

Rechtfertige deine Ideen und Meinungen.
Schreib ungefähr 130–150 Wörter **auf Deutsch**.

> You must justify your ideas and opinions by giving reasons and examples. Keep an eye on the word count though, and aim to write about 35 words for each bullet point.

> This activity carries 28 marks and you have four bullet points to respond to. You must answer each bullet point in a relatively equal way. Don't get carried away with one bullet point and run out of time or words for the other three.

2 Complete the task by writing your own answers to **all four** bullet points.
Complete your work on a separate sheet.

....

....

....

....

....

....   **(28 marks)**

Reading

Book festival

1 Read this report on your partner school's website about their reading festival.

> ● ● ●
>
> Wie jedes Jahr haben wir die Eltern und Geschwister der Schüler eingeladen, um das Lesefest mit uns zu feiern.
>
> Dieses Jahr haben wir beim Lesefest zum ersten Mal 20 Workshops angeboten. Die Lehrer und unsere zwei Gastautoren haben in kleinen Gruppen gearbeitet. Es gab Rollenspiele, Filme, Gedichte und Geschichten, alles zum Thema „Identität". Die Workshops waren sehr erfolgreich und sie werden in Zukunft wieder auf dem Programm stehen.
>
> Es gab auch den beliebten Lesewettbewerb. Dieses Jahr war die Aufgabe, ein Selfie beim Lesen zu machen. Die Fotos waren überraschend und oft sehr unterhaltsam. Man weiß jetzt genau, wo jeder liest!

Put a cross [x] in the correct box.

> Be aware of synonyms: words which are different but mean the same thing. For example you won't get *Mai* translated as 'May' for an answer option, but you might get a reference to its season: spring.

(i) The festival had taken place …

☐	**A** for the first time
☐	**B** at the end of the month
☐	**C** previously
☐	**D** as an experiment

(1 mark)

(ii) The school invites …

☐	**A** family members
☐	**B** former pupils
☐	**C** just existing pupils
☐	**D** just brothers and sisters

(1 mark)

(iii) The workshops were run by …

☐	**A** just the staff
☐	**B** staff and visitors
☐	**C** actors and poets
☐	**D** students

(1 mark)

(iv) The workshops were …

☐	**A** not a great success
☐	**B** missed off the programme
☐	**C** well received
☐	**D** well advertised

(1 mark)

(v) The competition revealed …

☐	**A** people's reading secrets
☐	**B** people's reading ability
☐	**C** nothing special
☐	**D** rather ordinary photos

(1 mark)

An author

2 You hear a young author introducing herself on Austrian radio. Listen to the author and answer the following questions **in English**.

> Each sentence of this recording has a question – do not lose concentration as you listen, or you will miss out on marks.

Listen to the recording

(a) Where does the author set her books?

.... **(1 mark)**

(b) Why has the author chosen this setting?

.... **(1 mark)**

(c) What will her readers gain from her books?

.... **(1 mark)**

Identity and culture   **Had a go** ☐   **Nearly there** ☐   **Nailed it!** ☐

Films

Cinema

1 Read this article by Patrick, your German exchange partner, about cinema.

> In der deutschen Tragikomödie *Honig im Kopf* geht es um einen ehemaligen Tierarzt, der an Alzheimer leidet. Til Schweiger spielte eine der Hauptrollen, und seine Tochter hatte auch eine Nebenrolle im Film.
>
> Meine Schwester geht nie ins Kino, weil das für sie Geldverschwendung ist. Sie meint, es ist viel billiger, Videos aus dem Internet herunterzuladen, aber das würde ich nie machen, weil das verboten ist.
>
> Letzte Woche habe ich im Stadtkino einen französischen Film gesehen, und die Geschichte hat mir ganz gut gefallen, weil sie sehr lustig und spannend war. Die Untertitel im Film waren nervig, aber es gab auch schöne Effekte und tolle Musik.

Answer the questions **in English**. You do not need to answer in full sentences.

(a) Who is the main character in *Honig im Kopf*?

.... **(1 mark)**

(b) What was unusual about the cast?

.... **(1 mark)**

(c) Give **one** reason why Patrick's sister does not approve of going to the cinema.

.... **(1 mark)**

(d) Why does Patrick not share her opinion?

.... **(1 mark)**

(e) Why did Patrick not greatly enjoy a film recently?

.... **(1 mark)**

> Read the questions carefully: question (e) asks why Patrick did **not** enjoy the film that much, not what he liked about it.

> You have to answer questions in English on both the Reading and the Listening papers, so watch out for these common pitfalls:
> - poor handwriting which cannot be read
> - writing too much detail
> - writing two items for a 1-mark question
> - writing only one item for a 2-mark question
> - copying random German words from the text/recording.

Television

TV programmes

1   Read Nadine's post on her homepage.

> ● ● ●
>
> Viele Seifenopern sind langweilig, meiner Meinung nach. Ich sehe mir lieber Sportsendungen an, weil das immer spannend ist. Im Internet gibt es im Moment einen tollen Krimi, den ich unbedingt sehen muss. Diese Serie verfolge ich seit letztem Jahr. Wenn man schlechter Laune ist, sind die besten Sendungen Komödien. Jeden Nachmittag sieht sich mein kleiner Bruder einen Zeichentrickfilm an, aber ich finde Zeichentrickfilme blöd.

Complete the gap in each sentence using a word from the box below.
There are more words than gaps.

similar	bored	this	thriller	boring	cross
cartoon	last	exciting	different	comedies	

> Complete the sentences you are confident of first and cross the word off the list – then come back to fill the other gaps once you have eliminated some of the words.

(a) Nadine finds sports programmes

....   **(1 mark)**

(b) She is watching a .... online.   **(1 mark)**

(c) She has been watching it since .... year.   **(1 mark)**

(d) Comedies are good when you are ....   **(1 mark)**

(e) Nadine has .... tastes to her brother.   **(1 mark)**

TV preferences

2   Hasan and Basil are discussing their TV preferences.

What do they enjoy about watching TV?

patient	films	modern
up-to-date	dated	soaps

Complete the sentences. Use the correct words from the box.

(a) Hasan enjoys relaxing and watching ....   **(1 mark)**

(b) Basil enjoys a .... way of watching TV

and being ....   **(2 marks)**

> Listen first for the gist – if you understand that, it will be much easier to identify the correct words when you listen for the second time.

Celebrations

Translation

1 Translate this passage **into English**.

> Wir feiern eine Hochzeit. Morgen heiratet meine Tante ihren Partner. Das ist wunderbar, weil sie ihn liebt. Gestern habe ich ein neues Kleid gekauft. Es ist toll, dass die ganze Familie zusammen ist.

When you translate a passage into English, don't make careless errors such as forgetting to translate a word or translating a sentence into a different tense from the original.

We are celebrating ....

....

....

....

.... **(7 marks)**

Make sure you have learned plenty of time words, such as *morgen* (tomorrow), *übermorgen* (the day after tomorrow) and *gestern* (yesterday). They give you a clue to the tense as well!

Don't forget to translate the declined adjective here, *neues*.

Party organiser

2 While listening to German radio you hear an interview with a party organiser, Herr Kreitling. What does he say?

Listen to the recording and put a cross [×] in the correct box for each question.

Listen to the recording

(i) Party organisers are …

☐	**A** no longer fashionable
☐	**B** not necessary
☐	**C** very expensive
☐	**D** growing in popularity

(1 mark)

(ii) They are particularly popular with … people.

☐	**A** busy
☐	**B** wealthy
☐	**C** injured
☐	**D** young

(1 mark)

(iii) You avoid stress if you … party planning.

☐	**A** do the
☐	**B** pay in advance for
☐	**C** delegate
☐	**D** ignore

(1 mark)

(iv) Parties these days have to be …

☐	**A** expensive
☐	**B** exciting
☐	**C** local
☐	**D** affordable

(1 mark)

(v) People who use party organisers are often …

☐	**A** confident
☐	**B** shy
☐	**C** original
☐	**D** lacking confidence

(1 mark)

Festivals

Weihnachten by Astrid Lindgren

1   Read the extract from the text.

Pelle has decided to leave the family home.

»Mama«, sagte Pelle, »wenn für mich Weihnachtskarten kommen sollten, sagst du dann wohl dem Briefträger, dass ich ausgezogen bin?«

Mama verspricht, es zu tun. Pelle geht zögernd wieder zur Tür.

»Pelle«, sagt Mama mit ihrer weichen Stimme, »Pelle – aber was sollen wir mit deinen Weihnachtsgeschenken machen? Sollen wir die nach Herzhausen hinunterschicken, oder kommst du und holst sie?«

»Ich will keine Weihnachtsgeschenke haben«, sagt Pelle mit zitternder* Stimme.

»Das wird aber ein trauriger Heiligabend. ... Alles, alles ohne Pelle.«

»Ihr könnt euch ja einen anderen Jungen anschaffen«, sagt Pelle mit zitternder Stimme.

»Nie im Leben«, sagt Mama. »Wir haben doch nur unseren Pelle so furchtbar lieb.«

> Split up compound words to aid your understanding. *Weihnachts + Karten* is easier to understand.

> Prefixes such as *hinauf* and *hinunter* simply mean 'up' and 'down', so focus on the main preposition (*unter/auf*).

> Be aware of cultural differences and customs in German-speaking countries. Presents are normally shared on *Heiligabend*.

* **zittern** = *to tremble*
  anschaffen = *to purchase, get*

Put a cross [x] in the correct box.

(i)   Pelle is expecting ...

☐	**A** tickets
☐	**B** friends
☐	**C** presents
☐	**D** post

(1 mark)

(ii) Pelle is ... to leave.

☐	**A** reluctant
☐	**B** happy
☐	**C** not going to
☐	**D** impatient

(1 mark)

(iii) Pelle ... his presents.

☐	**A** will collect
☐	**B** doesn't want
☐	**C** is taking
☐	**D** is undecided about

(1 mark)

(iv) Mama is ... Christmas Eve.

☐	**A** going away on
☐	**B** excited about
☐	**C** upset about
☐	**D** buying candles for

(1 mark)

(v) Mama thinks Pelle is ...

☐	**A** dreadful
☐	**B** annoying
☐	**C** irreplaceable
☐	**D** loud

(1 mark)

Holiday preferences

At the travel agency

1   Look at the role play task and read the student's response to the first **three** points.

Topic: Travel and tourist transactions

Instructions to candidates:

You are at a travel agency in Germany and are asking about a holiday. The teacher will play the role of the travel agent and will speak first.

You must address the travel agent as *Sie*.

You will talk to the teacher using the five prompts below.

- where you see – ? – you must ask a question
- where you see – ! – you must respond to something you have not prepared

> This sets the scene with the role play setup. It is your first indicator as to which register you need to use. Here, it is a formal situation at a travel agency, so **Sie** is required.

> You have **five** points which you need to **communicate** to your teacher in German. Repeating words from the card with a questioning intonation is not acceptable!

Task

Sie sind im Reisebüro in Deutschland und möchten in Urlaub fahren. Sie sprechen mit dem Manager / der Managerin.

> This repeats the setting in German – it may also contain vocabulary you can recycle, such as *möchten* and *Urlaub*.

1. Urlaub – Information

> Guten Tag. Wollen Sie in Urlaub fahren?

> Ja, ich interessiere mich für eine Woche Urlaub in Spanien.

> This could include place, time, length of stay, accommodation, getting there – you decide!

2. Unterkunft – was

> Welche Unterkunft möchten Sie haben?

> Ich möchte am liebsten in einem Hotel bleiben.

> Here you must give the accommodation where you want to stay.

3. !

> Haben Sie schon einmal einen Urlaub am Meer gemacht?

> Ja, ich war letzes Jahr in Korsika an der Küste.

> This is your unexpected question – here it is in the past tense, so make sure you answer in the same tense.

> Schön.

> It is important to concentrate to make sure you hear your teacher clearly in question 3! If you miss it, you would need to ask: *Können Sie das bitte wiederholen?* or *Wie bitte?*, but it really is better if you catch the question first time round.

Over to you!

2   Now look at the final two question prompts and make notes on how you would ask the questions. Then listen to the audio file before responding to all five prompts yourself.

4. ? Preis
5. ? Abendprogramm

Hotels

Booking a room

1 Look at the role play task and read the student's response to the first three points.

Topic: Travel and tourist transactions

Instructions to candidates:

You are booking a guest house room by phone. The teacher will play the role of the guest house manager and will speak first.

You must address the manager as *Sie*.

You will talk to the teacher using the five prompts below.

- where you see – ? – you must ask a question
- where you see – ! – you must respond to something you have not prepared

Task

Sie telefonieren mit einem Gasthaus in Deutschland. Sie wollen ein Zimmer reservieren.

1. Reservierung – Information

> Was wollen Sie reservieren?

> Ich will ein Doppelzimmer reservieren, bitte.

2. Ankunft – wann

> Wann kommen Sie an?

> Ich komme am Donnerstagabend an.

3. !

> Was wollen Sie zum Frühstück essen?

> Wurst mit Brot, bitte.

> Read the set-up information so you can start thinking about vocabulary and expressions which could come in handy for the task.

> In a Foundation role play you have: **one** unexpected question to respond to, so think about possibilities for this; and **one** question to ask, so prepare this using the information in prompt 5.

> This repeats the setting in German.

> Here you can state the type of room you want.

> You can prepare the day of your arrival in advance to ensure you give an accurate response.

> Listen for key words in the unexpected question. Here *Frühstück* and *essen* both lead you to respond with a food item – any will do!

Over to you!

SPEAKING TRACK 21

Listen to the recording

2 Now look at the final two prompts and make notes on how you would answer and ask them. Then listen to the audio file before responding to all five prompts yourself.

4. ? Transportmittel
5. ? Preis

Campsites

Campsite advert

1   Read this advert for a campsite.

Campingplatz Westerland

Besuchen Sie unseren neuen Campingplatz auf der Insel Sylt. Wir sind von Mai bis Oktober offen – Badetücher und Schlafsäcke können Sie hier mieten. Hier kann man sich sehr gut ausruhen, weil die Natur bei uns echt toll ist. Hier auf Sylt ist die Luft wunderbar frisch.

Ab zehn Uhr ist Ruhezeit auf dem Campingplatz. Niemand darf dann laute Musik hören – hier ist es herrlich im Freien und das will jeder genießen! Reservieren Sie heute einen Platz für Ihr Zelt oder ein Zimmer in unserem Bauernhof nebenan!

Complete the gap in each sentence using a word from the box below.
There are more words than gaps.

> outside   tent   blankets   nature   May   airfield
>
> quiet   caravan   towels   October   view

(a)   You can stay at the campsite from ....   **(1 mark)**

(b)   You can hire sleeping bags and ....   **(1 mark)**

(c)   The beautiful .... is particularly noteworthy.   **(1 mark)**

(d)   After ten o'clock everybody has to be ....   **(1 mark)**

(e)   You can book a pitch for a ....   **(1 mark)**

Campsite report

2   You hear a father talking about his holiday experiences on a German call-in radio show.

Listen to the caller and answer the following questions **in English**. You do not need to write in full sentences.

> For question (a), listen carefully – you may hear the cognate *beste* but you also need to pick up on what is 'the best' – it is not the campsite! Listen again to get the answer – just writing 'best' will not score you a mark.

Listen to the recording

(a)   Why does the caller return to the same campsite?

....   **(1 mark)**

(b)   Why are his children not keen on the campsite?

....   **(1 mark)**

(c)   How has their opinion affected the choice of the next holiday?

....   **(1 mark)**

Accommodation

Unterkunft

1 Lies den Ausschnitt aus der Unterkunftswebseite.

Hotel	Die Frühstücksauswahl hier ist fantastisch und riesig, und man hat nach dem Frühstück keinen Hunger mehr bis zum Abendbrot!
Gasthaus	Hier sind die Zimmer sehr bequem, und es sind frische Blumen auf dem Tisch. Das Haus hat schöne Möbel, und wir haben einen herrlichen Garten, wo Sie sich zu jeder Zeit entspannen können.
Bauernhof	Hier erleben Sie einen originellen Aufenthalt, weil Sie direkt neben den Kühen und den Enten übernachten. Dieser Urlaub ist besonders gut für Frühaufsteher und Tierfreunde!
Wohnblock	Mieten Sie eine Wohnung und wohnen Sie wie die Einwohner der Gegend! So können Sie die Umgebung richtig gut kennenlernen. Badetücher und Bettwäsche bringen Sie bitte selbst mit.

> Some German words are made up by combining smaller words – *Frühaufsteher* comes from *früh* (early) and *aufstehen* (to get up). Break down long words like this to aid your understanding.

Wo macht man das? Trag entweder **Hotel**, **Gasthaus**, **Bauernhof** oder **Wohnblock** ein. Du kannst jedes Wort mehr als einmal verwenden.

(a) Im .... wohnt man wie im eigenen Haus. **(1 mark)**

(b) Im .... kann man draußen chillen. **(1 mark)**

(c) Im .... bekommt man eine herzhafte Mahlzeit. **(1 mark)**

(d) Auf dem .... kann man morgens nicht lange schlafen. **(1 mark)**

(e) Im .... muss man für sich selber sorgen. **(1 mark)**

At the travel agency

2 While in Germany, you overhear an enquiry at the travel agency.

Listen to the recording and answer the following questions **in English**. You do not need to write in full sentences.

Listen to the recording

(a) What is the client's preferred accommodation?

.... **(1 mark)**

(b) Which aspect does she like about it?

....

> Listen for the compound noun in sentence (b), *Mehrbettzimmer*. Break it down – what do you think this means?

....

.... **(1 mark)**

(c) Which further aspect does she like?

.... **(1 mark)**

(d) Who does she also recommend it for?

.... **(1 mark)**

Holiday destinations

Holiday report

1   Read this report from an Austrian holiday website.

> ● ● ●
>
> ### Urlaubsziele
>
> Ob Sie einen Badeurlaub oder eine Stadtreise suchen, hier finden Sie alle Informationen über viele interessante Länder und Urlaubsregionen. Informieren Sie sich heute über die beliebtesten Urlaubsländer.
>
> Sie müssen nicht weit weg reisen, um Spaß zu haben! Österreich bietet tolle Möglichkeiten für jeden Urlauber. Egal, ob Sie etwas Aktives oder etwas Ruhiges suchen, Sie werden es in unserem Land finden.
>
> In Spanien gibt es viel Sonne und wunderschöne Strände. Die herrliche Küste und die kleinen Inseln gehören zu einem der attraktivsten und beliebtesten Reiseziele Europas. Die Landschaft fasziniert den Besucher – die Mischung aus Bergen, Seen und Städten ist fabelhaft.

Answer the following questions **in English**. You do not need to write in full sentences.

(a)   Where are the holidays advertised on this site?

.... **(1 mark)**

(b)   For what type of holidaymaker is Austria recommended?

.... **(1 mark)**

(c)   Which area is one of the most attractive holiday destinations in Europe?

.... **(1 mark)**

Beliebte Urlaubsziele

2   Du hörst dieses Interview mit der Besitzerin eines Reisebüros.

> See if you can identify the distractors as you listen first time round.

Füll die Lücke in jedem Satz mit einem Wort aus dem Kasten. Es gibt mehr Wörter als Lücken.

> | Unterkunft | Kosten | August | typische | Wetters | Dezember |
> |---|---|---|---|---|---|
> | Essens | erstaunlich | Deutschland | Leute | Küche | |

(a)   Die Informationen basieren auf einer Umfrage aus dem Monat

....   **(1 mark)**

(b)   Das .... Ziel der Sommerurlauber war es, schön braun zu werden.   **(1 mark)**

(c)   Das Land ist wegen des .... beliebt.   **(1 mark)**

(d)   Griechenland ist wegen der .... beliebt.   **(1 mark)**

(e)   Ein Nachteil von Griechenland ist die ....   **(1 mark)**

> Listen for key words to gain clues – here *Essen, Griechenland, nicht so appetitlich* all appear together. Which word from the box would sum this up?

Holiday experiences

Translation

Guided

1 Translate this passage **into English**.

> In den Winterferien fährt meine Familie Ski. Wir sind den ganzen Tag auf der Piste. Die Aussicht ist toll, wenn die Sonne scheint. Letztes Mal musste niemand ins Krankenhaus. Nächstes Jahr werde ich mit Freunden Urlaub machen.

In the winter holidays ....

....

We are ....

....

....

....

....

....

....

....

....

....

....

....

....

- Learn the different parts of the verbs *haben* (to have) and *sein* (to be) in the present tense – they are vital!
- Look at parts of words to help with the meaning of words such as *Aussicht* – *aus* (out) + *Sicht* (sight).
- Learn negative forms: *nicht* (not), *nie* (never), *kein(e)* (not a) and *niemand* (nobody).

(7 marks)

Urlaub planen

2 You hear a radio interview with Herr Metzger from a travel firm.

What does he say?

Listen to the audio twice – Herr Metzger has two sections of dialogue, with each one tackling a new aspect. Each section contains one of the answers you are looking for.

Choose the **two** correct answers.

A	His year abroad was a total success.	☐
B	He was forced to change his travel plans.	☐
C	He is always travelling for work.	☐
D	He runs holiday companies across the globe.	☐
E	His company provides information for young travellers.	☐

(2 marks)

Listen to the recording

Holiday activities

Urlaubsaktivitäten

1 Read the exam writing task and make brief notes of words or phrases you could use in your answer.

Schreib deiner Austauschpartnerin in England eine E-Mail über das Hotel, wo du arbeitest.

Schreib:

- **welchen Sport es im Hotel gibt**

- **warum es im Hotel nie langweilig ist**

- **was man abends im Hotel machen kann**

- **über Events nächstes Jahr.**

> The introduction sets the scene: here, you are working in a hotel and writing an email about activities in the hotel – start thinking about vocabulary and expressions you might like to use.

> You can use the present tense here: *es gibt einen Tennisplatz …* You can also mention what there isn't: *es gibt aber kein Schwimmbad.*

> Detail activities here which people can do at the hotel – use your imagination: *Jeden Montag gibt es eine Kunstklasse im Garten …*

> The bullet point uses the modal construction *machen kann*, so reflect this in your answer: *Abends kann man …*

> The words *nächstes Jahr* indicate you need to use the future tense or the present tense with a future time expression.

Schreib ungefähr 40–50 Wörter **auf Deutsch**.

Hallo Susan,

> Start your writing with a lower case letter, not a capital, i.e. **ich** as it follows from the comma.

....

....

....

....

....

Sample writing

Guided

2 Read this student's answer to the task and put the paragraphs in the correct order to match the bullet points above. Then prepare your own answer to the task on a separate page.

(a) Abends gibt es immer eine Disko – man kann hier bis spät tanzen.	1 c
(b) Nächstes Jahr wird ein Basketballspiel im Hotel stattfinden.	2 ....
(c) Hier gibt es viele Aktivitäten für alle. Man kann Tennis spielen oder im Freibad schwimmen gehen.	3 ....
(d) Wir haben auch Computer und Bücher, wenn das Wetter nicht so schön ist.	4 ....

Holiday plans

Alexander's plans

1 Read Alexander's letter.

> Lieber Opa,
>
> vielen Dank für das Geld. Es ist sehr nützlich, weil ich einen neuen Rucksack für den Urlaub brauche.
> Ich werde nächsten Monat mit meinem Freund Markus nach Frankreich und Spanien reisen.
>
> Ich freue mich sehr darauf! Markus hat ein Motorrad und die Reise wird viel Spaß machen. Wenn wir genug Geld haben, sind wir vier Wochen lang unterwegs.
>
> Wir werden zelten, um Geld zu sparen, und wir wollen in kleinen Hotels übernachten.
>
> Wir werden auch die Sehenswürdigkeiten besuchen.
>
> Ich werde dir viele Postkarten schicken!
>
> Viele Grüße von
>
> Alexander

(a) What is the letter about? Put a cross [×] in each one of the **three** correct boxes.

A	Alexander's grandfather has sent him a rucksack.	☐
B	Alexander plans to travel outside of Germany.	☐
C	He hopes to be away for at least two months.	☐
D	He will use his friend's transport.	☐
E	He will only stay on campsites.	☐
F	He will do some sightseeing.	☐
G	He will phone his grandfather.	☐

(3 marks)

Answer the following questions **in English**. You do not need to write in full sentences.

(b) Why might Alexander not be able to stay as long as planned?

.... **(1 mark)**

(c) What will Alexander send his grandfather when he is on holiday?

.... **(1 mark)**

Summer plans

2 You hear an interview with a student about her holiday plans on German radio.

Listen to the recording and answer the following questions **in English**. You do not need to write in full sentences.

Listen to the recording

LISTENING **TRACK 26**

(a) Give **two** reasons Saskia considers America an ideal destination.

.... **(2 marks)**

(b) Why does Saskia think she can stay with her aunt in America?

.... **(1 mark)**

(c) Why is Saskia keen to visit America soon? ....

.... **(1 mark)**

Had a go ☐ **Nearly there** ☐ **Nailed it!** ☐

Holiday problems

Translation

Guided

1 Translate this passage **into English**.

> Urlaube machen Spaß, wenn alles wie geplant läuft. Letzten Sommer haben sich unsere Nachbarn über ihr Hotel sehr beschwert. Meine Eltern fahren nie ins Ausland, weil sie die Sprache nicht sprechen und einen Unfall in einem fremden Land nicht haben wollen.

> Translate idioms naturally into English – German says 'make fun' (*machen Spaß*) but English just uses 'is/are fun'.

> You don't need to translate the word *sich* separately here, as it is just part of the verb *sich beschweren über* (to complain about).

Holidays are fun when everything goes to plan. ....

....

....

....

....

....

....

....

....

....

.... **(7 marks)**

> Read through your translation to check it makes sense and you haven't missed a word out by mistake.

An der Hotelrezeption

2 Du hast einen Sommerjob in einem Hotel in der Schweiz und hörst dieses Gespräch.

Wie ist es im Hotel? Trag entweder **gut**, **schmutzig**, **laut** oder **voll** ein. Du kannst jedes Wort mehr als einmal verwenden.

> Just note the first letter of the adjective while listening first time round so you don't get left behind – but don't forget to write it fully on your second listening.

(a) Das Zimmer ist .... **(1 mark)**

(b) Das Restaurant im Erdgeschoss ist .... **(1 mark)**

(c) Alle Zimmer in diesem Hotel sind .... **(1 mark)**

(d) Das andere Hotel ist .... **(1 mark)**

(e) Der Parkplatz ist im Moment .... **(1 mark)**

Listen to the recording

Asking for help

At the garage

1   Read this report about a garage from the trade journal for mechanics.

> Jeden Tag ist ein Kunde mit einer Panne zu uns gekommen und wollte sein Auto reparieren lassen.
> Früher habe ich allein hier gearbeitet, aber jetzt sind wir ein Team mit noch zwei Mechanikern und einem Assistenten. Viele Leute besitzen heute mindestens ein Auto und oft mehrere. Letztes Jahr hatten wir viel Arbeit, denn wir haben uns auf Motorräder spezialisiert.
> In Zukunft möchten wir auch eine Autoversicherung anbieten. Ich besuche morgen einen Kurs, um mich besser darüber zu informieren. Ich denke, das wird unseren Kunden überall viel helfen.

Put a cross [x] in the correct box.

(i) Customers' cars suffered particularly from …

☐	**A** breakdown
☐	**B** theft
☐	**C** flat battery
☐	**D** the cold

(1 mark)

(ii) The workshop employs …

☐	**A** just one person
☐	**B** five people
☐	**C** two people
☐	**D** four people

(1 mark)

(iii) These days, many people …

☐	**A** share cars more
☐	**B** can only afford one vehicle
☐	**C** own more than one vehicle
☐	**D** often hire a car

(1 mark)

(iv) The workshop was successful due to …

☐	**A** focusing on one area
☐	**B** people owning more cars
☐	**C** its location
☐	**D** advertising

(1 mark)

(v) The boss is keen to …

☐	**A** offer cheap car hire
☐	**B** learn about something new
☐	**C** remain exactly as it is
☐	**D** run mechanics courses

(1 mark)

Emergency call

2   While training with the mountain rescue team in Switzerland, you hear this emergency phone call.

Listen to the phone call and answer the following questions **in English**. You do not need to write in full sentences.

Listen to the recording

(a) Where is the caller?

.... **(1 mark)**

(b) Why did she go for a walk?   [Make sure you answer this question as 'why', not 'where'.]

.... **(1 mark)**

(c) What situation does she now find herself in?

.... **(1 mark)**

Transport

Emil und die Detektive by Erich Kästner

1   Read the extract from the text.

Emil has just arrived in Berlin and is on the trail of the man who stole his money on a train earlier.

> **Straßenbahnlinie 177**
>
> Und die Straßenbahn fuhr. Und sie hielt. Und sie fuhr weiter. Emil las den Namen der schönen breiten Straße. Er fuhr und wusste nicht, wohin. Im andern Wagen saß ein Dieb. Ein fremder Herr hatte ihm zwar einen Fahrschein geschenkt. Doch nun las er schon wieder die Zeitung.
>
> Die Stadt war so groß. Und Emil war so klein. ... Vier Millionen Menschen lebten in Berlin und keiner interessierte sich für Emil Tischbein.

> Look out for verbs made from familiar nouns to help your understanding.
> *Geschenk* = 'present' and *geschenkt* = 'gave'.

Answer the following questions **in English**. You do not need to write in full sentences.

(a) Give **one** movement the tram made.

.... **(1 mark)**

(b) How is the street described?

.... **(1 mark)**

(c) Where was Emil heading?

.... **(1 mark)**

(d) Give **one** example of something the stranger had done.

.... **(1 mark)**

(e) Why did Emil feel he was insignificant?

.... **(1 mark)**

Public transport in Hamburg

2   You hear this advert for Hamburg public transport while on holiday there.

What are its key advantages?

Listen to the recording

Listen to the recording and put a cross [×] in each one of the **three** correct boxes.

A	buses only in the city centre	☐
B	city and regional buses available	☐
C	all bus routes have a 24-hour service	☐
D	no underground travel required	☐
E	no car required to get around	☐
F	very good value for money	☐
G	users recommend the service	☐

> If you are really stuck with the choice of a correct answer, use your common sense to help you. Which is more likely to be true: **A** buses only in the city centre, or **B** city and regional buses available?

(3 marks)

Travel

Unterwegs

1 Übersetze **ins Deutsche**.

Work your way through each sentence in turn, making sure you do not miss any words out in your translation.

> **Guided**

(a) My father finds cars practical.

Mein Vater ....

.... **(2 marks)**

Think about the verb ending in the third person (*er*), as you are talking about what somebody else finds, not what you find.

> **Guided**

(b) I prefer to go by bus.

Ich ....

.... **(2 marks)**

gehen = to go/walk, *fahren* = to go/drive

Use *gern*, *lieber* and *am liebsten* to express activities you enjoy, prefer and like doing most. Just add them after the verb: *Ich singe gern* = 'I like singing'.

(c) The traffic in my town is really loud.

.... **(2 marks)**

(d) Last week we drove on the motorway.

....

....

.... **(3 marks)**

Learn your prepositions carefully – they are crucial small words which you cannot afford to miss out.

(e) We played cards, because it is fun.

....

....

.... **(3 marks)**

If you use *weil* here, remember to put the verb at the end of the clause. *Denn* is an alternative for 'because' and it doesn't alter the word order.

Unterwegs

2 Übersetze **ins Deutsche**.

> **Guided**

My mother had a dreadful journey to the office yesterday. Her car broke down next to the petrol station. She has to cycle now, while the car is in the garage. I wish that fewer people would drive cars, as the public transport here is so good.

- German articles need to match their noun: *mein Vater*, *meine Mutter* and *mein Kind*.
- You cannot always translate an expression word for word: use *eine Panne haben* to say a 'car has broken down'.
- Subordinating conjunctions *während* (while), *dass* (that), *wenn* (if) and *als* (when) all send the following verb to the end of the clause. Make sure you do too!

Meine Mutter hatte gestern eine

schreckliche Fahrt ....

....

....

.... **(12 marks)**

Directions

Wegbeschreibungen zur Party

1 Lies Lennys Wegbeschreibungen.

> ✉
>
> Ich organisiere eine Party am 23. Mai bei mir! Meine Adresse ist Reisstraße 34 und es gibt eine Bushaltestelle nur zwei Minuten entfernt. Ihr könnt also mit dem Bus Nummer 124 zur Party fahren.
>
> Ihr könnt natürlich auch mit dem Rad zum Fest kommen, weil die Fahrradwege prima sind. Fahrt an der Schule links und dann über die Brücke. Nehmt die zweite Straße rechts und fahrt geradeaus bis zur Straßenkreuzung.
>
> Unser Haus liegt auf der rechten Seite zwischen der Kirche und der Grünanlage.

> Instructions can be in any one of the 'you' forms: *du, Sie* and *ihr*. Make sure you recognise them in a reading passage.

Füll die Lücke in jedem Satz mit einem Wort aus dem Kasten. Es gibt mehr Wörter als Lücken.

> | schlechte | richtig | Park | Dom | Auto | falsch |
> |---|---|---|---|---|---|
> | überqueren | Haustier | Adresse | fotografieren | gute |

> Look out for the preposition *ohne* (without) in sentence (a) – it is important!

(a) Man kann das Haus ohne .... erreichen. **(1 mark)**

(b) Radfahren ist eine .... Alternative. **(1 mark)**

(c) Man muss einen Fluss .... **(1 mark)**

(d) Wenn man an der Kreuzung ankommt, ist man .... gefahren. **(1 mark)**

(e) Lenny wohnt neben dem .... **(1 mark)**

Directions

2 Herr Kojik is talking to his son, Alfred.

What does he say?

Listen to the recording and complete the sentences by putting a cross [×] in the correct box for each question.

> Make learning cards for key expressions – draw a direction on one side and write the German on the other side. You can then test yourself to help widen and reinforce your vocabulary bank.

Listen to the recording

(i) The instruction is to …

☐	**A** go left at the supermarket
☐	**B** go past a shop
☐	**C** carry straight on
☐	**D** turn right

(1 mark)

(ii) Alfred should have …

☐	**A** turned left
☐	**B** turned right
☐	**C** stopped at the hospital
☐	**D** turned left at the school

(1 mark)

(iii) Alfred needs to …

☐	**A** turn around
☐	**B** wait for his dad
☐	**C** go up to the lights
☐	**D** go round the corner

(1 mark)

(iv) The snack bar is beside the …

☐	**A** zebra crossing
☐	**B** square
☐	**C** lights
☐	**D** bridge

(1 mark)

Eating in a café

Café Istanbul

1   Read this posting about a local café.

> ● ● ●
>
> Café Istanbul ist ein neues Café am Markt. Die Kellner sind alle sehr freundlich und das Café ist toll für junge Leute.
>
> Das Essen schmeckt sehr gut. Die türkischen Spezialitäten sind besonders lecker, und das berühmte Lammschaschlik ist auch echt preiswert.
>
> Man kann auch einen wunderbaren Kaffee in dem Café trinken, und die Atmosphäre ist sehr locker. Leider dürfen keine Hunde ins Café.

> Highlight any items of vocabulary you do not know in this passage – look them up in an online dictionary and make a note of them to learn. The words here are key vocabulary.

Answer the following questions **in English**. You do not need to write in full sentences.

(a) What sort of people would particularly like this café?

.... **(1 mark)**

(b) Give **one** reason why the kebab is recommended.

.... **(1 mark)**

(c) What is the only negative thing mentioned about the café?

.... **(1 mark)**

Eating out

2   An Austrian radio show has done a survey about eating out.

Listen to Sabine's interview for the survey and answer the following questions **in English**. You do not need to write in full sentences.

> Use the information given before the activity as well as the questions themselves to help orientate yourself as to what you will be listening to.

Listen to the recording

(a) What does Sabine particularly enjoy about eating in a restaurant?

.... **(1 mark)**

(b) Give **two** reasons why she does not enjoy self-service restaurants.

....

.... **(2 marks)**

(c) How does she justify the expense of eating at a restaurant?

.... **(1 mark)**

(d) Give **one** occasion which is worth going to a restaurant for.

.... **(1 mark)**

Eating in a restaurant

Im Restaurant

1   Read the writing task and underline any elements which you think are key.

> In the exam, you are given a choice of two scenarios for this writing task – you need to choose **one** of them to base your writing on. You will not have time to change your mind halfway through your work, so make sure you choose wisely!

Deine Freundin Alessa schickt dir Fragen über deinen Restaurantbesuch.

Schreib eine Antwort an Alessa.

> Here you are writing a reply to a friend, so use the familiar *du* form.

Du **musst** über diese Punkte schreiben:

- **was du gern isst**

> The first point is a gentle start – present tense, and an opportunity to choose details which will show off vocabulary you know about that topic.

- **was für ein Problem es gab**

> This is asking for a negative issue with the visit – this can be anything from dirty forks, to noisy people or a mouse … use your imagination within the extent of your German knowledge!

- **wie der Restaurantbesuch war und warum**

> Any bullet point containing *warum* is asking you for your opinion. Use *weil* or *denn* to justify the opinion.

- **deine Pläne für den nächsten Restaurantbesuch.**

> Words such as *Pläne* and *nächsten* trigger the future tense – make sure this is what you use!

Schreib ungefähr 80–90 Wörter **auf Deutsch**.

Sample writing

> Guided

2   Read this student's answer to the task and put the paragraphs in the correct order to match the bullet points above. Then prepare your own answer to this task on a separate page.

(a) Der Abend war aber ein ganz großer Erfolg, weil die Kellner alle sehr lustig und sympathisch waren.

(b) Im Restaurant esse ich sehr gern italienisches Essen, weil das so lecker schmeckt, aber ich gehe auch manchmal gern in ein indisches Restaurant.

(c) Nächste Woche werde ich mit der Klasse in die Pizzeria gehen, weil unser Klassenlehrer seinen fünfzigsten Geburtstag feiern wird und er uns alle eingeladen hat.

(d) Als Vorspeise habe ich eine Kartoffelsuppe gegessen, aber sie war echt salzig und sie hat furchtbar geschmeckt.

Correct order:

1   b   2 ....   3 ....   4 ....

Shopping for food

Online-Supermarkt

1   Lies diesen Ausschnitt von einer Online-Supermarkt-Webseite.

● ○ ○	
Äpfel	Es gibt verschiedene Sorten, also probieren Sie doch einen süßen oder einen sauren Leckerbissen! So werden Sie Ihren Lieblingsapfel finden!
Bananen	Unsere Bananen sind besonders klein, also ideal für das Pausenbrot. Wir importieren sie mit dem Schiff aus Spanien, und sie schmecken süß und lecker.
Pflaumen	Backen Sie gern? Eine köstliche Torte können Sie mit diesen frischen Pflaumen aus Österreich backen! Das perfekte Rezept finden Sie <u>hier</u> auf unserer Webseite.
Trauben	Wir haben grüne, rote und schwarze Trauben für Sie, weil sie bei jedem Alter immer beliebt sind! Wenn Sie auch Traubensaft suchen, dann klicken Sie <u>hier</u>.

> To find the answers, you need to look for related words in the texts. For example, statement (a) mentions *verschiedene Farben – Farbe* is a key word meaning 'colour', so although you won't find this exact word in a text, you can look for colour-related words (*grün, rot, schwarz*) to lead you to the answer.

Was ist das? Trag entweder **Äpfel**, **Bananen**, **Pflaumen** oder **Trauben** ein. Du kannst jedes Wort mehr als einmal verwenden.

(a) .... haben verschiedene Farben.   **(1 mark)**

(b) .... sind nützlich für die Schule.   **(1 mark)**

(c) .... schmecken nicht alle gleich.   **(1 mark)**

(d) .... sind ideal zu Kaffee und Kuchen.   **(1 mark)**

(e) .... findet man auch in einem Getränk.   **(1 mark)**

Market stall work experience

2   You hear a radio interview with Raul about his work experience at the market.

> Even if you don't catch the key words, the gist of a text can lead you to the answer. Raul says he felt *erschöpft*, and then he continues to give a reason for this, from which you can infer he was exhausted/tired, as he had to get up so early.

LISTENING TRACK 32

Listen to the recording

Listen to the interview and answer the following questions **in English**. You do not need to write in full sentences.

(a) How did Raul feel after his work experience week?

....   **(1 mark)**

(b) Why couldn't he go straight to the market stall each morning?

....   **(1 mark)**

(c) What did Raul particularly enjoy at the stall?

....   **(1 mark)**

(d) What did Raul find challenging?

....   **(1 mark)**

(e) What could attract Raul to the job of market trader?

....   **(1 mark)**

Opinions about food

Gesund essen

1   Lies die Beiträge auf einer Webseite über gesundes Essen.

> ● ● ●
>
> **Ben:** Als ich jünger war, aß ich zu viele Süßigkeiten, und ich trank immer mit meinen Freunden große Flaschen Cola sowie Energiegetränke. In der Grundschule hatte ich riesige Probleme mit den Zähnen, und ich musste deshalb meine Gewohnheiten ändern, um sie zu schützen. Ich sollte wohl einige Kilos abnehmen, aber das gelingt mir nie, denn ich mache nicht gern Diät.
>
> **Mina:** Zu Hause koche ich meistens leckere Mahlzeiten ohne viel Salz oder Fett. Ich studiere Sport und wir trainieren viermal in der Woche, daher darf ich nur einmal in der Woche Alkohol trinken. Wenn man Sportlerin sein möchte, muss man sich vor allem an eine ausgeglichene Diät halten, weil man sonst zu viele Kilos zunehmen würde und das wäre eine Katastrophe für das Trainingsprogramm.

Beantworte die Fragen **auf Deutsch**. Vollständige Sätze sind nicht nötig.

> Even if you can work out the answer, you need to be able to express it in German – writing key words in English will not score you any marks. This is also telling you that you do not need to write in full sentences.

(a)   Ben hat zu viel von welcher Zutat gegessen?

> Sweets and bottles of cola are both sweet items, but writing *süß* or copying the items from the text does not answer the question. You need to know the word for the ingredient 'sugar'. Learning key vocabulary will help you to tackle this!

....   **(1 mark)**

(b)   Warum hat Ben seine Diät geändert?

> Use an *um ... zu* phrase or the preposition *wegen* to give a reason here.

....   **(1 mark)**

(c)   Warum wird Ben nicht abnehmen?

> There are two options for this answer – choose the **one** you are confident with.

....   **(1 mark)**

(d)   Wie isst Mina?

> This question has moved on to Mina's text – you can check your answers to Ben's text now if you like, or do them all together at the end.

....   **(1 mark)**

(e)   Was findet Mina am wichtigsten für ihre Zukunft?

....   **(1 mark)**

Buying gifts

My photo description

1   Look at the picture-based task for the photo and read this student's answers to the first two bullet points. Then prepare your own answers to the remaining bullet points.

Schau dir das Foto an und sei bereit, über Folgendes zu sprechen:

- **Beschreibung des Fotos**

Das Bild zeigt ein wunderbares Geschäft, wo man schöne Andenken vom Urlaub kaufen kann. Ich denke, dass die Frau im Bild in diesem Geschäft arbeitet. Sie trägt warme Kleidung, weil es wahrscheinlich kalt ist. Sie lächelt und holt ein Souvenir vom Regal. Vielleicht hat jemand das gerade gekauft und sie muss es jetzt als Geschenk einpacken.

- **Deine Meinung zu Geschenken**

Mir ist es wichtig, Geschenke zu geben, und ich weiß, dass ich immer sehr gern Geschenke bekomme. Wenn ein Freund oder ein Familienmitglied Geburtstag hat, sollte man ihm etwas geben. Solche Geschäfte wie das im Foto sind meiner Meinung nach ideal für ein Reisegeschenk, und ich würde wahrscheinlich hier viele Geschenke kaufen.

- **Ein Geschenk, das dir nicht gefallen hat**

- **Ob du in Zukunft deine Geschenke im Geschäft oder im Internet kaufen wirst**

- **!**

> At Higher tier you have four bullet points you can prepare for and !, meaning you must answer an unexpected question.

> Your first task is to say something factual about the photo, i.e. what you can see. You could **describe** where it is set, who is in it, what they are wearing, or anything else you can **see** in the photo.

> This student has used the subordinating conjunction *wo* here (*ein Geschäft, wo*) and *diesem Geschäft* rather than *dem Geschäft* – both simple ways to raise the level.

> Here you need to give your opinion. Words such as *Meinung, meinen, denken, finden* all indicate the teacher is looking for an opinion. You can use the present tense for this.

> The use of the dative phrase *mir ist es wichtig* and a *dass* clause both show confidence in using the German language.

> This question is your opportunity to showcase your past tense knowledge – try to include a pluperfect too if you can: *gewünscht hatte.*

> This next question moves on to the future tense, so make sure you reply in this tense: *werde … kaufen.*

> Impress by also adding some conditional short forms: *könnte* (could), *wäre* (would be) and *hätte* (would have).

> If you don't understand the question, just ask politely: *Können Sie das bitte wiederholen?* or *Wie bitte?*

2   Look at the Answers section on page 124 to read and listen to the student's answers to the task in full.

> If you don't understand a question and ask to hear it again, remember that you can only ask **twice** for something to be repeated.

Weather

Der Weltenwanderer: Zu Fuß um die halbe Welt by Gregor Sieböck

1 Read the extract from the text.

Gregor is recounting his trekking experiences in Peru.

> Bald entdeckte ich die riesige Goldmine neben der Inkastraße. In der Ferne zog ein Gewitter auf, und die Inkastraße verschwand wieder einmal im hohen Punagras. Die Nebelschwaden wurden dichter.
>
> Der Nebel war nun so dicht geworden, dass ich kaum zehn Meter weit sehen konnte, das Donnergrollen kam immer näher und ich irrte verloren im Gras umher. Regentropfen begannen zu fallen. Wo sollte ich hier einen trockenen Platz für das Zelt finden?
>
> Weit und breit gab es nur schmutziges Moorland, und wo es nicht nass war, gab es das meterhohe Punagras. Da sah ich sie plötzlich: eine etwa zwei Quadratmeter große Rasenfläche! Unglaublich! Ich baute rasch das Zelt auf, kochte ein einfaches Abendbrot und ging völlig erschöpft in meinen Schlafsack.

> Don't be put off by separable verbs in different tenses – *zog … auf* is the imperfect tense of *aufziehen*, meaning here 'to appear'.

> Some words might be unfamiliar, but part of the word might be recognisable, so look carefully: *Gras* in the second paragraph of the text is a cognate, and *Punagras* is just a specific type of grass. Similarly, with *Nebelschwaden* and *Donnergrollen* – it is the familiar first part of the word that is key.

Put a cross [x] in the correct box.

(i) In the first paragraph the weather …

☐	**A** remained the same
☐	**B** deteriorated
☐	**C** improved
☐	**D** was kind

(1 mark)

(ii) Gregor became …

☐	**A** disorientated
☐	**B** cold
☐	**C** ill
☐	**D** tired

(1 mark)

(iii) It began to …

☐	**A** rain
☐	**B** snow
☐	**C** clear
☐	**D** dry

(1 mark)

(iv) Camping was difficult due to …

☐	**A** too much choice
☐	**B** Gregor's height
☐	**C** the terrain
☐	**D** wildlife

(1 mark)

(v) Gregor finally felt … about his situation.

☐	**A** dreadful
☐	**B** slightly happy
☐	**C** badly
☐	**D** grateful

(1 mark)

Places to see

Town

1 The German exchange class has made a podcast about their town.

Listen to the recording and put a cross [×] in the correct box for each question.

Listen to the recording

Part (a)

(i) You can have a snack …

☐	**A** by the exit
☐	**B** in the basement
☐	**C** in the exhibition
☐	**D** on the first floor

(1 mark)

> Learn basic vocabulary to help you with listening passages – if you are confident with locations in a building, this question will be easy for you and you can move straight on to the next one.

(ii) You can't take a photo on your mobile at the gallery because …

☐	**A** it might damage the paintings
☐	**B** it encourages crowding
☐	**C** the postcards are cheap
☐	**D** there is not enough light

(1 mark)

(iii) The town has …

☐	**A** many inhabitants
☐	**B** wide streets
☐	**C** modern buildings
☐	**D** spooky secrets

(1 mark)

The interview continues.

Listen to the recording

Part (b)

(i) The trip to the countryside …

☐	**A** is not recommended
☐	**B** will take place next Saturday
☐	**C** should be pre-booked
☐	**D** always has spaces

(1 mark)

(ii) The bus trip happens …

☐	**A** occasionally
☐	**B** every week
☐	**C** every afternoon
☐	**D** during fine weather

(1 mark)

(iii) Ivan considers his town to be …

☐	**A** ugly
☐	**B** dull
☐	**C** ordinary
☐	**D** worth visiting

(1 mark)

> You need to listen for adjectives here – *malerisch*, *schön* and *interessant* all give you big clues to this answer, as does the final idiom used: *eine Reise wert sein*!

At the tourist office

What to do in town

1 Read the information leaflet from the Bremen tourist office.

> Jedes Jahr kommen viele Touristen nach Bremen und sie kommen oft noch einmal wieder.
>
> Sie finden hier preiswerte Unterkünfte, aber während des Weihnachtsmarktes sollten Sie unbedingt im Voraus buchen, weil Hotels und auch Jugendherbergen schnell ausgebucht sind.
>
> Mit der „Erlebniscard Bremen" kann man billiger mit öffentlichen Verkehrsmitteln fahren, und die können Sie online oder bei uns im Verkehrsamt bestellen. Außerdem bekommt man mit dieser Karte Ermäßigungen fürs Theater, für Führungen usw.
>
> Im Schnoorviertel finden Sie allerlei interessante Läden, wo Sie traditionelle Andenken oder Geschenke für Freunde und Familie kaufen können.
>
> Jeder Besucher wird in den vielen verschiedenen Museen etwas Interessantes finden. Vergessen Sie bei der Planung aber nicht, dass die meisten Museen montags geschlossen sind.

(a) What is the text about? Put a cross [×] in each one of the **three** correct boxes.

A	Many people visit Bremen more than once.	☐
B	Bremen is a new town.	☐
C	Lots of visitors come at Christmas time.	☐
D	You can always find accommodation available.	☐
E	Public transport is cheap for everybody.	☐
F	You can save money through a special card.	☐
G	Bremen does not have a theatre.	☐

(3 marks)

Answer the following questions **in English**. You do not need to write in full sentences.

(b) Who might be especially attracted to the *Schnoorviertel*?

.... **(1 mark)**

(c) What vital piece of information is given at the end?   Be specific in your answer here!

.... **(1 mark)**

Plans for the day

2 Hannes and his friends are talking about activities in town. What do they say?
Listen to the recording and put a cross [×] in each one of the **three** correct boxes.

A	I am walking today.	☐
B	I am going on public transport.	☐
C	I want to be outside.	☐
D	I am going shopping.	☐
E	I have got a street plan.	☐
F	I am sending postcards.	☐
G	I value architecture.	☐

(3 marks)

Listen to the recording

> You won't hear the statements **A–G** in order, but you will hear what each person says in turn, and then you need to choose the correct name for each statement.

Describing a town

Erik's town

1 You hear this audio diary on the radio.

What do you find out about Erik's town?

Listen to the recording and complete the sentences by putting a cross [x] in the correct box for each question.

Listen to the recording

(i) Erik's new home seems …

☐	**A** the same
☐	**B** lucky
☐	**C** strange
☐	**D** familiar

(1 mark)

> He does use the word *glücklicherweise* but don't interpret this as meaning his home is lucky in any way; he does say he feels he is *im Ausland*, so this should lead you to the correct answer.

(ii) The size of Erik's new town compared to his old town is …

☐	**A** not mentioned
☐	**B** smaller
☐	**C** the same
☐	**D** bigger

(1 mark)

> You need to pick up on words related to the size of the town, which Erik describes through the number of inhabitants. Don't assume you will hear actual size-related words for the town itself for this answer.

(iii) Erik is particularly impressed by the …

☐	**A** sports facilities
☐	**B** students
☐	**C** public transport
☐	**D** location

(1 mark)

(iv) Erik finds the universities are advantageous for …

☐	**A** older people
☐	**B** young adults
☐	**C** all people
☐	**D** very young children

(1 mark)

> You won't hear the exact words from the answer options, but listen for the category of people who benefit from the university. Can you infer which group they belong to?

(v) Erik does not advise a visit to the town centre …

☐	**A** ever
☐	**B** on a Monday morning
☐	**C** on a Saturday afternoon
☐	**D** on a Saturday night

(1 mark)

Describing a region

Matching questions and answers

1   Match the student's replies (A–E) to the teacher's questions (1–5). Draw lines to link them.

> Your teacher will start this part of the Conversation, and you need to make sure you respond to the questions with as much detail as you can, justifying your opinions and using a good range of tenses.

1   Wo ist dein Wohnort?

A   Am Samstag bin ich zuerst mit dem Bus in die Stadt gefahren, um neue Sportschuhe zu kaufen. Danach habe ich meine Freunde im Café getroffen und wir sind anschließend zusammen zum Skatepark gefahren. Das hat Spaß gemacht, obwohl das Wetter sehr kalt war.

2   Was kann man in deiner Gegend machen?

B   Ich wohne in einem Dorf im Nordwesten von England in der Nähe von Liverpool. Die nächste Stadt in der Gegend heißt St Helens und sie hat ungefähr hunderttausend Einwohner.

3   Was hast du am Wochenende in deiner Gegend gemacht?

C   Als Tourist hier muss man unbedingt das Glasmuseum in St Helens besuchen, weil das sehr interessant ist. Ich würde auch einen Besuch an der Küste empfehlen, weil die Landschaft dort sehr eindrucksvoll ist. Es wäre auch gut, an einem Abend einmal ins Theater zu gehen.

4   Was würdest du einem Touristen in deiner Gegend empfehlen?

D   Ich würde einen Freizeitpark in dieser Gegend bauen, weil der uns hier im Moment fehlt. Junge Leute würden das super finden, besonders wenn man den Park einfach mit dem Bus von überall her erreichen könnte.

5   Was möchtest du an deiner Gegend ändern?

E   Hier im Dorf hat man viele Möglichkeiten: man kann im Park Fußball spielen oder nach St Helens fahren und ins Stadion gehen, um ein Rugbyspiel zu sehen. Hier in der Gegend kann man auch ins Kino oder Theater gehen, und in der Stadt gibt es viele Restaurants und Nachtlokale.

> Include conjunctions such as *wo* and *weil* in your spoken work to help raise the level. Remember, the verb goes to the end of the clause with both these conjunctions.

Answering questions on a topic

2   How would you respond to the teacher's five questions above? Prepare your own answer to each one, using the student's answers to help you.

Then turn to the Answers section and listen to one student's answers. Pay particular attention to the pronunciation of cognates such as *England*, *Tourist* and *Theater*.

Had a go ☐   Nearly there ☐   Nailed it! ☐

Tourism

Translation

1 Translate this passage **into English**.

> Meine Eltern fahren gern ins Ausland. Sie schreiben gern Postkarten. Ich fahre nie zu einem Flughafen, weil ich nicht gern fliege. Letztes Jahr bin ich mit der Bahn in die Schweiz gefahren. Im Sommer mache ich eine Busreise an die Küste.

My parents ....

....

They ....

....

I ....

....

Last ....

....

In ....

....

(7 marks)

> Translate *gern* as 'like' doing something, so *gern schreiben* means 'like writing'.

> Watch out for the tense in this sentence – it is not in the present tense.

> In German, you can use the present tense to talk about the immediate or near future, just like in English!

Holiday report

2 You hear a holiday report on the radio.

What three things are said about the holiday?

Listen to the recording and put a cross [×] in each one of the **three** correct boxes.

A	The accommodation is amazing.	☐
B	The area is not very nice.	☐
C	There are too many cars on the roads.	☐
D	It is a noisy area.	☐
E	There is a trip planned.	☐
F	They must wear walking shoes.	☐
G	There will be a change of temperature.	☐

Listen to the recording

> Make sure you have learned your quantity words: *wenig* = 'not much', *viel* = 'lots'.

> Don't be tripped up by the comparative forms: *kalt – kälter – am kältesten*.

(3 marks)

Countries

Translation

1 Translate this passage **into English**.

> Wenn man ein fremdes Land besucht, muss man das im Voraus planen. Man kann zum Reisebüro gehen oder alles im Internet recherchieren. Ich empfehle aber auch einen Reiseführer, weil er sehr nützlich ist. Als ich letztes Jahr in die Türkei gefahren bin, habe ich die Reise geplant und das hat sich gelohnt.

- Use known connections to help with meaning: *im Voraus* is connected to *vorher* (before) and *vor* (in front of). Use the rest of the sentence to confirm its meaning here.
- Translate the German *man* as 'you', 'one' or 'people' – depending on the context of the sentence.

If you visit a foreign country ....

....

....

....

....

....

....

....

....

....

....

.... **(7 marks)**

Foreign travel

2 You listen to two reports on the radio about foreign travel.

Listen to the reports and answer the following questions **in English**. You do not need to write in full sentences.

(a) What does the first reporter say about herself? Give **two** details.

....

.... **(2 marks)**

(b) How does her education help in Spain?

.... **(1 mark)**

(c) Why does the Swiss man prefer going abroad?

.... **(1 mark)**

(d) What does he regret about Switzerland?

.... **(1 mark)**

School subjects

Schulfächer

1 Übersetze **ins Deutsche**.

> All German nouns have capital letters – don't forget to use them when you translate.

(a) I find maths difficult.

> **Guided**

Ich finde ....

.... **(2 marks)**

> If you can't remember the word for 'difficult', change it around and say 'not easy': *nicht einfach*. The meaning remains the same so the translation is valid.

> **Guided**

(b) I don't like science.

Ich ....

.... **(2 marks)**

> Watch out for the negative here: you could use *nicht mögen* or *nicht gern machen*.

(c) We have geography every Wednesday.

....

.... **(2 marks)**

(d) Yesterday I got a good grade in chemistry.

....

.... **(3 marks)**

(e) I like art because it is interesting.

....

....

....

.... **(3 marks)**

> *Weil* is a subordinating conjunction, so the following verb goes to the end of the clause.

Schulfächer

2 Übersetze **ins Deutsche**.

> Express the negative with *nicht* or *kein(e)*: *keine Sprachen lernen* or *Sprachen nicht lernen*.

> **Guided**

> This year I have chosen Italian and French. At primary school, we didn't learn any foreign languages. My class also does Spanish and we are travelling to Madrid soon. I would love to study Latin because that is useful for university.

Dieses Jahr habe ich Italienisch und Französisch gewählt. In

....

....

....

....

.... **(12 marks)**

> Use subjunctive forms to express uncertainty or wishes for the future: *würde gern* (would like), *könnte* (might, could), *wäre* (would be).

> In the exam, you will have more space than this. Continue your answer here on lined paper.

Had a go ☐   Nearly there ☐   Nailed it! ☐

Opinions about school

Esma's school

1   Read your exchange partner's blog about school.

> ● ● ●
>
> Die Lehrer sind meistens nett, aber die Kunstlehrerin ist sehr streng und echt mies. Mathe finde ich ziemlich schwierig und gestern hatte ich Angst, weil wir eine Klassenarbeit schreiben mussten.
>
> Ich finde, dass es fair ist, wenn es in einer Schule viele Regeln gibt. Rauchen ist verboten und das finde ich gut. Aber ich finde es dumm, dass Kaugummis in Klassenzimmern nicht erlaubt sind.
>
> Ich finde es ärgerlich, dass wir so viele Hausaufgaben bekommen. Nach der Schule tanze ich lieber oder ich spiele im Schulorchester. Hausaufgaben sind langweilig und ich mache sie später am Abend.

Put a cross [x] in the correct box.

> If you are not sure which answer is correct, try to decide which ones are definitely wrong to limit your options.

(i)   Esma finds the art teacher ... the other teachers.

☐	**A** the same as
☐	**B** nicer than
☐	**C** funnier than
☐	**D** not as nice as

(1 mark)

(ii)   Yesterday Esma found maths ...

☐	**A** easy
☐	**B** funny
☐	**C** scary
☐	**D** dull

(1 mark)

(iii)   Esma's opinion of the school rules is ...

☐	**A** mixed
☐	**B** totally positive
☐	**C** totally negative
☐	**D** not clear

(1 mark)

(iv)   Esma thinks the amount of homework was ...

☐	**A** well judged
☐	**B** troublesome
☐	**C** helpful
☐	**D** acceptable

(1 mark)

(v)   Esma does homework ...

☐	**A** the next morning
☐	**B** straight away
☐	**C** after activities
☐	**D** rarely

(1 mark)

Moritz's school

2   You hear a report about Moritz's experience of school.

Listen to the report and answer the following questions **in English**. You do not need to write in full sentences.

Listen to the recording

(a)   Give **one** problem Moritz's school had. .... (1 mark)

(b)   Why was it difficult to learn properly in class? .... (1 mark)

(c)   Why did Moritz change schools? .... (1 mark)

> Keep your answers short and relevant. Check that you really have answered the question.

School day

Toms Schultag

1 Lies Toms E-Mail über den Schultag.

> ✉
>
> Nach dem Frühstück gehe ich zehn Minuten zu Fuß zur Schule und plaudere vor dem Schulbeginn auf dem Schulhof mit meinen Freunden.
>
> Wir haben um halb zehn eine kleine Pause. Dienstag ist mein Lieblingstag, weil wir eine Doppelstunde Erdkunde haben.
>
> Ich esse jeden Tag zu Hause zu Mittag, weil das Essen in der Schulkantine mir nicht sehr schmeckt. Nach der Schule gibt es oft Musik- und Sportgruppen, aber ich gehe lieber nach der letzten Stunde sofort nach Hause zu unserem Wohnblock, um mich an den Computer zu setzen.

Füll die Lücke in jedem Satz mit einem Wort aus dem Kasten aus. Es gibt mehr Wörter als Lücken.

> | | | | | | |
> |---|---|---|---|---|---|
> | lecker | nie | hasst | liebt | zehn | Nähe |
> | gern | unappetitlich | Samstags | Bibliothek | neun | |

> Check you know your 12-hour times in German – *halb acht* = 'half past seven'.

(a) Tom wohnt in der .... der Schule.   **(1 mark)**

(b) Die erste Pause ist um .... Uhr dreißig.   **(1 mark)**

(c) Tom .... Geografie.   **(1 mark)**

(d) Tom findet das Essen in der Schule ....   **(1 mark)**

(e) Nach der Schule ist Tom .... zu Hause.   **(1 mark)**

Teaching routine

2 Frau Grün is giving details about her routine as a teacher. What does she say?

Listen to the recording and complete the sentences by putting a cross [×] in the correct box for each question.

Listen to the recording

(i) In the first lesson Frau Grün is teaching …

☐	**A** class 9
☐	**B** class 8
☐	**C** different classes
☐	**D** a favourite class

(1 mark)

(ii) Frau Grün regards breaktime as an opportunity to …

☐	**A** relax
☐	**B** deal with pupils
☐	**C** work
☐	**D** make calls

(1 mark)

(iii) In the afternoon Frau Grün …

☐	**A** relaxes at home
☐	**B** goes for a walk
☐	**C** stays at school
☐	**D** exercises

(1 mark)

Had a go ☐   **Nearly there** ☐   **Nailed it!** ☐

Types of schools

German schools

1   Read Dajana's letter about school.

> Ich besuche ein Gymnasium mit etwa eintausend Schülern und Schülerinnen. Die Uni nebenan ist dreimal so groß.
>
> Als kleines Kind war ich in der Grundschule sehr glücklich, weil das immer so viel Spaß gemacht hat.
>
> Die ersten Tage am Gymnasium waren furchtbar. Das Schulgebäude war so groß. Einmal konnte ich das Labor gar nicht finden und ich habe eine Strafarbeit bekommen, weil ich nicht pünktlich im Physikunterricht angekommen bin!
>
> Jetzt bin ich in der zehnten Klasse und ich leide unter dem Druck, weil ich lieber Sport im Freien treibe, als gute Noten in Klassenarbeiten zu bekommen. Ich brauche aber sehr gute Noten, weil ich ein gutes Abitur machen muss, wenn ich später als Tierärztin arbeiten möchte.

(a)   What is the text about? Put a cross [×] in each one of the **three** correct boxes.

A	Dajana's school has fewer students than the university.	☐
B	Dajana was unhappy at her previous school.	☐
C	When she was younger, Dajana liked school a lot.	☐
D	Dajana didn't get on with people at primary school.	☐
E	Dajana found the transition to secondary school easy.	☐
F	Dajana has never got into any trouble at school.	☐
G	Dajana was once late for class.	☐

(3 marks)

Answer the following questions **in English**. You do not need to write in full sentences.

> These questions refer to the final paragraph – don't go back to look earlier for the answers.

(b)   What does Dajana find problematic about school?

....   **(1 mark)**

(c)   Why does Dajana need to do well at school?

....   **(1 mark)**

An English school

2   Sonja has made a podcast to send to her old school in Germany. Listen to the recording and answer the following questions **in English**. You do not need to write in full sentences.

Listen to the recording

(a)   Give **two** aspects of the English school which Sonja dislikes.

....

....   **(2 marks)**

(b)   What does Sonja miss about her old school in Germany?

....   **(1 mark)**

(c)   Who is Sonja impressed by at the English school?

....   **(1 mark)**

(d)   Which aspect of the English school system does Sonja find to be the worst?

....   **(1 mark)**

School facilities

Translation

1 Translate this passage **into English**.

> Heute haben wir Chemie im Labor. Ich mache lieber Sport in der Turnhalle. Unsere Schule ist toll, weil das Essen in der Kantine lecker schmeckt. Am Dienstag habe ich eine Dose Cola im Kunstraum getrunken. Das ist verboten!

Guided

> Watch out for false friends! *Dose* is not a 'dose'. Context gives you the real meaning here!

Today we have chemistry in the laboratory. I prefer ....

....

....

....

....

....

....

....

....

....

....

.... **(7 marks)**

The 'third teacher'

2 You hear a radio interview with Frau Beton from an architect's practice.

What does she say?

Listen to the recording

Choose the **two** correct answers.

A	Each year group has its own individual space.	☐
B	The year groups share a main entrance.	☐
C	The buildings all look the same.	☐
D	Three elements contribute to the learning process at school.	☐
E	Schools will be much better designed in future.	☐

(2 marks)

> Use any of the listening passages in this Workbook to help improve your pronunciation – repeat sentences after the speaker to compare how you sound. The tapescripts are all available online to double-check against.

School rules

Schulregeln

> You are being tested here on your ability to *communicate* a response to each of the bullet points. To do this you need to be secure in your knowledge of German and be able to apply the words and structures *accurately*.

Du magst die Schulordnung an deiner Schule nicht.

Schreib einen Artikel über die Schulordnung.

Du **musst** über diese Punkte schreiben:

- **warum du die Schulordnung nicht magst**

> A *warum* question means you need to justify your opinion – here, why you do not like the school rules.

- **welche Regel dich geärgert hat**

> This has now moved on to the past tense as you need to write about an example of a school rule you **have** experienced.

- **was du verändern möchtest**

> If you come across *würde* or *möchte*, it will be the conditional you need to use – here, you need to explain how you **would** change the rules.

- **deine Pläne für eine Schulordnung in der Zukunft.**

> The future tense is needed here – make sure you use it.

Rechtfertige deine Ideen und Meinungen.

> Expand your answer to each bullet point by giving a reason to justify your opinion, within the word limit.

Schreib ungefähr 130–150 Wörter **auf Deutsch**.

Sample writing

> Check your written work through at the end for spelling and grammar mistakes. Use the Grammar section at the end of this book to help get your grammar up to speed by the time the exams arrive.

Guided

1 Read this student's answer to the task and put the paragraphs in the correct order to match the bullet points above. Then prepare your own answer to this task on a separate page.

(a) Könnten die Regeln für die Schuluniform nicht flexibler sein? Es wäre toll, wenn wir zum Beispiel einmal pro Woche unsere eigene Kleidung tragen könnten. Meiner Meinung nach würden alle Schüler dann viel besser lernen.

(b) Ich hasse die Schulordnung, weil ich sie unfair und zu streng finde. Als Jugendliche müssen wir zur Schule gehen, weil das Pflicht ist, aber es macht uns keinen Spaß, wenn wir endlosen Regeln folgen müssen.

(c) Wir werden keine Schuluniform tragen und werden jeden Freitag schulfrei haben. Es wird keine Strafarbeiten mehr geben und das wird die Schule verbessern.

(d) Letzte Woche habe ich in der Schule meine Sportschuhe verloren. Obwohl meine Eltern am Anfang des Halbjahrs telefonisch erklärten, dass wir kein Geld für neue Schuhe bis Ende des Monats haben, habe ich trotzdem eine Strafarbeit bekommen.

Correct order:

1 b   2 ....   3 ....   4 ....

Pressures at school

Der Tag, an dem ich cool wurde **by Juma Kliebenstein**

1   Read the extract from the text.

Martin is describing his first day at secondary school.

> Jedenfalls erzähle ich zu Hause nicht so gerne von der Schule,
> weil Mama und Papa nicht verstehen würden, dass ich dort
> ständig mit den FabFive Stress habe.
>
> Ich weiß noch genau, wie ich damals mit meiner Mutter in der
> großen Aula saß, zusammen mit vielleicht hundert anderen,
> und **darauf gewartet habe**, in meine neue Klasse zu gehen.
>
> Mann, hab' ich mich unwohl gefühlt. Die Farbe des Hemdes hat
> sich ziemlich mit meiner roten Brille gebissen, und außerdem
> sah es ziemlich knapp aus. ...
>
> Irgendwie hatte ich schon **geahnt**, dass das nicht so toll für
> mich laufen würde.

warten auf = 'to wait
for', *darauf gewartet
haben* = 'waited for'.

keine Ahnung = 'not a clue',
so use this to work out
what the past participle
geahnt means. Looking for
connections is always a
useful strategy to use!

Put a cross [×] in the correct box.

(i)   At home, Martin doesn't talk
      about his ...

☐	**A** family
☐	**B** class
☐	**C** success
☐	**D** hobbies

(1 mark)

(ii) Martin has ... had trouble at
      secondary school.

☐	**A** never
☐	**B** always
☐	**C** occasionally
☐	**D** hardly

(1 mark)

(iii) Martin was waiting in the ...

☐	**A** foyer
☐	**B** classroom
☐	**C** canteen
☐	**D** hall

(1 mark)

(iv) Martin felt ... on his first day.

☐	**A** excited
☐	**B** happy
☐	**C** uncomfortable
☐	**D** confident

(1 mark)

(v) Martin was ... by his feelings.

☐	**A** not surprised
☐	**B** not concerned
☐	**C** surprised
☐	**D** reassured

(1 mark)

Primary school

An der Grundschule

1 Lies die Beiträge zum Forum.

Ömer	Die Grundschullehrer waren sehr nett und lustig. Sie waren nie schlecht gelaunt und sie haben uns tolle Lieder sowie Instrumente beigebracht.	**Jens**	Die Grundschule war toll, weil ich oft gezeichnet habe. Ich hatte ein großes Federmäppchen mit vielen bunten Filzstiften und Bleistiften. Kunst ist immer noch mein Lieblingsfach.
Liza	Es war besser, weil wir keine Hausaufgaben machen mussten. Nach der Schule konnten wir Fußball spielen oder fernsehen. Ich habe damals gern Bilder gemalt, aber jetzt fotografiere ich lieber.	**Halina**	In der Grundschule gab es keinen Stress, weil wir keinen Stundenplan hatten. Jeden Tag konnte man stundenlang auf dem Schulhof spielen. Das war super klasse.

Wer sagt das? Trag entweder **Ömer**, **Liza**, **Jens** oder **Halina** ein. Du kannst jedes Wort mehr als einmal verwenden.

(a) .... war froh, nachmittags frei zu haben. **(1 mark)**

(b) .... hat es gefreut, entspannt zu sein. **(1 mark)**

(c) .... war stolz auf sein Etui. **(1 mark)**

> A scan of the text can help with this style of activity – it won't take long to find out who mentions any words connected to music.

(d) .... hat die musikalischen Angebote gut gefunden. **(1 mark)**

(e) .... hat jetzt ein neues Hobby. **(1 mark)**

Primary school memories

2 The actor Waltraud Schmidt is reflecting on her time at primary school.

Listen to the recording and answer the following questions **in English**. You do not need to write in full sentences.

(a) What did Waltraud do all day?

.... **(1 mark)**

b) What did she enjoy once a week?

.... **(1 mark)**

(c) What did she not enjoy?

.... **(1 mark)**

(d) What was her Friday treat?

.... **(1 mark)**

> Make sure what you write on the exam paper does actually provide the answer to the question.

Success at school

School

1 Read the article in the prospectus about how this school celebrates success.

> Das Karl-Huber-Gymnasium ist eine freundliche Schule am Stadtrand – wir haben tolle Schüler(innen) im Alter von elf bis achtzehn Jahren.
>
> Wir feiern oft ihre guten Noten – das heißt, die Mathe- oder Deutschlehrer(innen) zum Beispiel geben den Schülern/Schülerinnen aus der Klasse einen kleinen Preis. Das findet jeden Freitag in der Aula statt.
>
> Einmal im Herbst gibt es einen Wettbewerb an der Schule – die Gewinner(innen) bekommen am ersten Schultag ihre Medaillen.

Part (a)

Answer the following questions **in English**. You do not need to write in full sentences.

> Don't be put off by feminine forms given in brackets: *Schüler(innen)* is here to acknowledge both genders of pupil, as each one has its own word in German.

(i) What is the age of the oldest pupils at the school?

.... **(1 mark)**

(ii) When are good grades celebrated?

.... **(1 mark)**

(iii) What event takes place once a year?

.... **(1 mark)**

> If you can't remember what *Wettbewerb* means, look at the next part of the sentence. Pupils are given medals – when might this happen?

The article continues.

Part (b)

> Wir organisieren oft Feste, um die kreativen Fächer zu feiern. Zum Beispiel haben wir im März unser Lesefest und im Juli gibt es das große Musikfest.
>
> Das Karl-Huber-Gymnasium ist stolz auf seine Schüler(innen). Es gibt hier immer etwas zu feiern: im Klassenzimmer, auf dem Sportplatz und im Labor.

(i) When is the reading festival?

.... **(1 mark)**

(ii) Give an example of **one** area in the school where pupils can gain success.

.... **(1 mark)**

> Don't refer back to Part (a) here – this section is completely separate.

Class trips

Translation

1 Translate this passage into English.

> Jede Klasse geht einmal im Jahr auf Klassenfahrt.
> Die meisten Reisen finden in Deutschland statt, aber manche
> Schüler fahren auch ins Ausland. Ich würde gern nach
> Amerika reisen, aber ich weiß, dass das zu teuer ist.
> Letztes Jahr freute ich mich echt sehr auf die Woche an der
> Küste, aber ich war dann am Reisetag krank.

> Remember words such as *jeder* (each) and *mancher* (some).

Every class goes on a class trip once a year.

Most trips ....

....

....

....

....

....

....

....

....

> You often don't need to translate the word for 'the' into English, even though the German needs it.

Class trips

2 Your German exchange partner is talking about what his friends think of class trips.

What does he say about them?

Listen to the recording and put a cross [×] in each one of the **three** correct boxes.

A	has a trip in the summer	☐
B	has a trip at Christmas	☐
C	is not keen on class trips	☐
D	is staying in a hotel	☐
E	is not going on a trip	☐
F	is going to the coast	☐
G	has a trip to the forest	☐

Listen to the recording

(3 marks)

School exchange

Switzerland–Scotland exchange

1   Read the postings sent from Swiss teenagers who are on an exchange programme in Scotland.

Anna	Ich mag es hier nicht. Ich vermisse meinen Hund – ich komme nicht gut mit meiner Partnerin aus.
Kevin	Mein Austauschpartner wohnt auf einer Insel. Wir fahren jeden Tag mit dem Boot zur Schule! Nachmittags schwimmen wir in der See.
Sophie	Die Schule beginnt erst um neun Uhr, und das finde ich das Beste. Ich mag auch den Unterricht hier, weil die Labors und die Computerräume sehr modern sind.
Shiyan	Ich mag das Essen hier sehr – jeden Abend dürfen wir Pizza vor dem Fernseher essen. Das darf ich zu Hause nie!

die See = 'sea'
der See = 'lake'

Who says what about themselves? Enter either **Anna**, **Kevin**, **Sophie** or **Shiyan**. You can use each person more than once.

(a) .... is most pleased with the school timetable.   **(1 mark)**

(b) ....'s partner does not live on the mainland.   **(1 mark)**

(c) .... is enjoying mealtimes.   **(1 mark)**

(d) .... does not have a good relationship with their partner.   **(1 mark)**

(e) .... has different rules at home.   **(1 mark)**

(f) .... is impressed by the facilities.   **(1 mark)**

Poland–Germany exchange

2   You hear a radio interview with Frau Weglarz, the coordinator for a Poland–Germany exchange programme. Listen to the interview and answer the following questions **in English**. You do not need to write in full sentences.

Listen to the recording

(a) Since when has Frau Weglarz been responsible for the exchange?

....   **(1 mark)**

(b) What did pupils succeed in doing to make friends?

....   **(1 mark)**

(c) What were the visitors able to promote while in Germany?

....   **(1 mark)**

(d) Give **one** advantage of the exchange for the visitors.

....   **(1 mark)**

(e) What hope do students from both countries share?

....   **(1 mark)**

Weltfrieden = 'world peace'; this was mentioned in the introduction to the recording and *in einer friedlichen Welt* is mentioned at the end. Make a note of words such as *der Krieg* (war) and *der Frieden* (peace).

School events

At school in Germany

1 Look at the role play card and read the student's response to the first three bullet points.

Topic: School

Instructions to candidates:

You are visiting your German exchange partner.
The teacher will play the role of the exchange partner and will speak first.

You must address your exchange partner as *du*.

You will talk to the teacher using the five prompts below.

> In a Higher role play you have **one** unexpected question to respond to, so think about the possibilities for your scenario here. You also have **two** questions to ask, so prepare them using the information in prompts 4 and 5.

- where you see – ? – you must ask a question
- where you see – ! – you must respond to something you have not prepared

Task

Du bist mit deinem deutschen Austauschpartner/deiner deutschen Austauschpartnerin in der Schule in Deutschland.

1. Schulevent – Beschreibung

> Was für Events gibt es an deiner Schule?

> Im Sommer findet immer ein großes Sportfest statt.

> Details here could be the event type, when it takes place, where it takes place, who it is aimed at – you decide!

2. Schulevents – Meinung

> Wie findest du Schulevents?

> Ich finde Schulevents toll, weil sie interessant und spannend sind.

> Here you must give an **opinion** about school events. This can be positive, negative or a mixture of both!

3. !

> Wie war das Event letztes Jahr?

> Es hat viel Spaß gemacht und ich habe eine Medaille gewonnen.

Over to you!

TRACK 45

Listen to the recording

2 Now look at the remaining two prompts below and make notes on how you would ask the questions. Then listen to the audio file before responding to all five prompts yourself.

> Avoid just repeating the prompt questions – phrase the question in your own words.

| 4. ? Events – wann |
| 5. ? Events – Meinung |

Future study

Further study plans

1 Read this email from Samira about her plans for studying after school.

> ✉
>
> Gestern habe ich die letzte Prüfung für die Mittlere Reife gemacht und ich bin jetzt nervös auf die Ergebnisse! Ich brauche sehr gute Noten, um auf das beste Gymnasium in der Gegend zu gehen. Meine Eltern glauben, dass ich das Abitur dann mit einer hohen Durchschnittsnote machen werde.
>
> Als ich jünger war, wollte ich Krankenschwester werden, aber jetzt denke ich anders. Letztes Jahr fand ich das Arbeitspraktikum bei einem Tierarzt faszinierend, und ich habe mich entschieden, lieber mit Tieren als mit Menschen zu arbeiten.
>
> Nach der Schule möchte ich an der Uni Tiermedizin studieren. Das Studium wird einige Jahre dauern, und ich will lieber in eine andere Stadt ziehen, weil das billiger ist. So werde ich sicher neue Erfahrungen machen, und ich finde es wichtig, selbstständig zu werden.

Answer the following questions **in English**. You do not need to write in full sentences.

(a) Why do Samira's parents want her to go to the grammar school?

.... **(1 mark)**

(b) What made Samira change her career plans?

.... **(1 mark)**

(c) Why does Samira want to study away from home?

.... **(1 mark)**

Ein Weg zum Abitur

2 Du hörst dieses Interview mit einem Lehrer an einer Realschule.

Füll die Lücke in jedem Satz mit einem Wort aus dem Kasten aus. Es gibt mehr Wörter als Lücken.

Listen to the recording

> | lockerer | Reisen | Möglichkeiten | reich | Lehrer |
> |---|---|---|---|---|
> | Gymnasium | Arbeit | manche | Prüfungen | strenger | alle |

(a) Kinder, die an das .... gehen könnten,

besuchen heute eine Realschule.   **(1 mark)**

(b) Die Realschule ist .... als das

Gymnasium.   **(1 mark)**

> Make sure you understand the statements when you read them before you listen – underline words which you think are key.

(c) Nach der letzten Prüfung hat ein Realschüler viele

....   **(1 mark)**

> Listen for a cognate here which is a synonym for the answer.

(d) .... Schüler machen Abitur.   **(1 mark)**

(e) Wenn man nicht auf die Uni geht, kann man trotzdem interessante

.... machen.   **(1 mark)**

Jobs

Job choices

1 Read this article about choosing a job.

> ● ● ●
>
> ## Was mache ich als Beruf?
>
> Jedes Jahr haben viele Jugendliche diese Frage. Die Antwort ist leider gar nicht einfach, weil die Auswahl an Möglichkeiten für den Weg in die Arbeitswelt so groß ist. Und sie wird immer größer.
>
> Die Verwandten haben schon an der Grundschule gefragt: „Was willst du später als Beruf machen, Danilo?" „Möchtest du mit Tieren arbeiten, oder lieber mit Menschen, mein liebes Kind?"
>
> Aus Büchern und dem alltäglichen Leben kennen Kleinkinder schon Berufe wie Lehrer(in), Busfahrer(in) und Arzt/Ärztin, also wählen sie wahrscheinlich einen davon, damit solche unerwünschten Fragen aufhören.

> You can work out **unerwünschten** by breaking the word down: **wünschen** = to wish and **un-** indicates a negative.

Answer the following questions **in English**. You do not need to write in full sentences.

(a) Why do students often not know what they want to do after school?

.... **(1 mark)**

(b) Name one area of work that relatives suggest young children might choose to work in.

.... **(1 mark)**

(c) Why might a young child choose a doctor as a potential job?

.... **(1 mark)**

People's jobs

2 Your Austrian exchange partner is talking about how his friends are finding their jobs.

What does he say about them?

Listen to the recording and put a cross [×] in each one of the **three** correct boxes.

A	likes the clients	☐
B	is looking for a new job	☐
C	finds the job tiring	☐
D	works in a bakery	☐
E	has a good salary	☐
F	works with animals	☐
G	likes the work hours	☐

(3 marks)

Professions

Translation

1 Translate this passage **into English**.

> Meine Mutter ist Tierärztin. Sie arbeitet in der Stadtmitte. Ihre Arbeit gefällt ihr, weil sie gern anderen Leuten hilft. Letzte Woche hat unser Hund einen Unfall gehabt. Morgen gehen wir zum ersten Mal wieder in den Park.

> Be aware of irregular feminine forms for jobs – *der Arzt/die Ärztin.*

My mother is a vet. She works ....

....

....

....

....

....

.... **(7 marks)**

> You may be familiar with the expression *gefällt mir* (I like), so you should have no problem translating it here with the pronoun changed to *ihr* (her).

> Numbers come in cardinals (for counting) and ordinals (for dates): *eins (erster), zwei (zweiter), drei (dritter).* See the Grammar section, page 108.

My job

2 Hugo and his friends are talking about their jobs.

What do they say?

> Listen carefully to the whole recording before making your selection.

Listen to the recording and put a cross [×] in each one of the **three** correct boxes.

A	I am looking for a new job.	☐
B	I work in a factory.	☐
C	I am an office worker.	☐
D	I like working with customers.	☐
E	I have just started my job.	☐
F	I am well paid.	☐
G	I work in the countryside.	☐

(3 marks)

Listen to the recording

Job wishes

Future options

1 Read this article in a student magazine.

Es ist heute bei der Jugend nicht mehr so beliebt, auf ein Gymnasium und dann sofort auf die Uni zu gehen. Viele Schüler(innen) bevorzugen eher einen Ausbildungsplatz als Mechaniker(in) oder Klempner(in).

Einige junge Leute studieren jedoch an der Uni in der Hoffnung, in Zukunft einen guten Beruf mit einem hohen Gehalt zu bekommen.

Es gibt eine große Auswahl an Berufen, die für alle Schüler(innen) geeignet sind, aber sie müssen sich den Beruf natürlich selber aussuchen. Manche Schüler(innen) wollen

Parkarbeiter(innen) oder Bauern/ Bäuerinnen werden, weil sie meinen, dass sie auch im Winter oder bei schlechtem Wetter lieber im Freien als in einem Gebäude mit Klimaanlage arbeiten würden.

Nach dem Abitur arbeiten manche Schüler(innen) zuerst freiwillig bei einer Wohltätigkeitsorganisation. Sie helfen vielleicht in einem Heim für Obdachlose oder alte Menschen und lernen dabei vieles, was für die Arbeitswelt echt nützlich sein wird. Solche Arbeitserfahrung wird jedem Arbeitgeber imponieren.

> die Hoffnung (hope)

Answer the questions **in English**. You do not need to write in full sentences.

> The questions are in the same order as the text, so keep moving through the passage as you answer each question.

(a) Why don't all students opt for university?

.... **(1 mark)**

(b) What is the appeal of studying at university?

.... **(1 mark)**

(c) Why should students be able to find a job?

.... **(1 mark)**

(d) Why might students prefer an office or shop job?

.... **(1 mark)**

(e) What is the main advantage of doing voluntary work?

.... **(1 mark)**

Opinions about jobs

Views on jobs

1 Read Susi and Elif's views about jobs in this magazine article.

> **Susis** Chefin geht allen auf die Nerven, weil sie ziemlich gemein und sehr ehrgeizig ist.
>
> Diese Chefin erzeugt eine schlechte Atmosphäre am Arbeitsplatz, aber manchmal kann man das nicht vermeiden, denkt Susi, die schon seit elf Jahren in der Marketingabteilung arbeitet.
>
> Ehrlich gesagt würde Susi lieber weniger Geld verdienen und bessere Arbeitsbedingungen haben, aber sie kann sich nach so langer Zeit nicht
>
> vorstellen, sich um eine neue Stelle zu bewerben. Sie ist nämlich froh, dass sie berufstätig ist und dass die Arbeitsstunden nicht zu lang sind, obwohl sie ab und zu bis spät arbeiten muss.
>
> Im Gegensatz dazu arbeitet **Elif** bei der Post, wo er Schichtarbeit machen muss. Er möchte viel lieber in einer Fabrik oder in einem Büro arbeiten, wo er wenigstens normale Arbeitsstunden hätte. Der einzige Vorteil ist, dass die Arbeit gut bezahlt ist, und das ist ihm wichtig.

(a) What is the text about? Put a cross [×] in each one of the **three** correct boxes.

A	Susi doesn't have any friends at work.	☐
B	Susi's boss is not an easygoing person.	☐
C	Susi thinks poor management is always avoidable.	☐
D	Susi is trying hard to improve her job situation.	☐
E	Susi has had the same job for many years.	☐
F	Susi has to do overtime occasionally.	☐
G	Susi has to clean the office every day.	☐

(3 marks)

Answer the following questions **in English**. You do not need to write in full sentences.

(b) What is wrong with Elif's job? .... **(1 mark)**

(c) What makes his job bearable? .... **(1 mark)**

A new job

2 Ben is being interviewed on local radio about his first day working at a department store.

Listen to the recording and answer the following questions **in English**. You do not need to write in full sentences.

Listen to the recording

(a) What was Ben's task on his first day at work?

.... **(1 mark)**

(b) What did Ben's boss do which Ben disapproved of?

.... **(1 mark)**

(c) Give **two** advantages of Ben's new job.

....

.... **(2 marks)**

(d) Why will Ben stay with the job?

.... **(1 mark)**

Job adverts

Restaurant job advert

1 Read the job advert.

> ### Bewerben Sie sich heute bei uns!
>
> Sind Sie fleißig und freundlich? Sie möchten in einem modernen Restaurant mit tollen Kollegen und unter guten Arbeitsbedingungen arbeiten?
>
> Wir suchen Kellner/innen für unser neu eröffnetes italienisches Restaurant neben dem Dom. Erfahrung ist nicht wichtig.
>
> Wir sind stolz auf unseren internationalen Restaurantbetrieb, und Ihr Ziel als Kellner/in wird es sein, unsere Kunden immer nach bestem Können zu bedienen.
>
> Kommen Sie heute vorbei, um ein Bewerbungsformular abzuholen. Schicken Sie uns das Formular mit Lebenslauf spätestens bis Montag, den 12. März, wieder zurück.

> Don't be put off by *Können* used as a noun here – it just means 'ability'.

> proud   experience   send   food   prospects   cathedral
>
> conditions   smart   station   ashamed   collect

Complete the gap in each sentence using a word from the box below.
There are more words than gaps.

(a) This job offers good work .... **(1 mark)**

(b) The restaurant is near the .... **(1 mark)**

(c) You don't necessarily need .... **(1 mark)**

(d) The restaurant is .... of its service. **(1 mark)**

(e) You have to .... the application form personally. **(1 mark)**

A job advert

2 You hear a dialogue about jobs between Zac and Caitlyn from a German soap opera.

What is said in the conversation?

Listen to the recording and put a cross [×] in each one of the **three** correct boxes.

A	Zac is well suited to the job advertised.	☐
B	Zac's mum works at a travel agency.	☐
C	Zac would have to make a sacrifice to accept the job.	☐
D	The job would use up all of Zac's free time.	☐
E	Zac has failed all his exams once.	☐
F	Zac's work ambitions have not changed since he was young.	☐
G	Zac wants to work for his aunt.	☐

(3 marks)

Applying for a job

Job search

1 Read the writing task and underline any elements which you think are key.

Dein Freund Sergio fragt dich nach deiner Arbeitssuche.

Schreib eine Antwort an Sergio.

Du **musst** über diese Punkte schreiben:

> Don't just write the first thing that comes into your head regarding 'Job search' – you need to tailor your writing to match the bullet points.

- **was für eine Stelle es ist**

> Use vocabulary you are confident of here – remember, German has different forms for male and female jobs: *der Lehrer/die Lehrerin*.

- **Arbeitserfahrung**

> Use the past tense here – you can use the perfect (*haben/ sein* + past participle) and the imperfect (*war/hatte*).

- **warum diese Stelle**

> The question word *warum* means 'why' – knowing your question words is vital for all the exam papers!

- **wo du in Zukunft arbeiten wirst.**

> You are writing about future jobs here, so adjectives such as *prima*, *interessant* and *toll* could come in handy.

Schreib ungefähr 80–90 Wörter **auf Deutsch**.

> Practise writing tasks as you revise, so you know approximately how many lines your handwriting takes to reach 80–90 words.

Sample writing

Guided

2 Read this student's answer to the task and put the paragraphs in the correct order to match the bullet points above. Then prepare your own answer to this task on a separate page.

(a) Letztes Jahr habe ich im Sportverein gearbeitet, aber dieses Jahr gibt es leider keine Ferienjobs dort.

(b) Nach der Schule werde ich Arbeit suchen, die draußen ist, denn das finde ich besser als drinnen zu arbeiten. Ich werde deshalb nicht in einem Büro arbeiten.

(c) Ich bewerbe mich im Moment um einen Job als Bademeister im Schwimmbad in der Stadtmitte.

> Adding details to the bullet points (where, when, how) will help to ensure you reach the word count. Here, the student has said where the pool is.

(d) Diese Stelle würde mir sehr gut passen, weil wir im Sommer nicht in den Urlaub fahren werden. Deshalb könnte ich dann viel arbeiten.

> Use the Grammar section at the back of this book to double-check you are secure with the different points of grammar while you are revising for writing skills.

Correct order:

1   c   2 ....   3 ....   4 ....

Job interview

At the job centre

1 Look at the role play card and read the student's response to the first three points.

> Don't overcomplicate your answers; the role play is the opening part of the speaking exam and there is plenty of opportunity elsewhere for showing off your German to its full extent!

Topic: Future plans

Instructions to candidates:

You are looking for a job at the job centre. The teacher will play the role of the manager and will speak first.

You must address the manager as *Sie*.

You will talk to the teacher using the five prompts below.

- where you see – ? – you must ask a question
- where you see – ! – you must respond to something you have not prepared

Task

Sie sind in Österreich und suchen einen Job beim Arbeitsamt. Sie sprechen mit dem Manager/ der Managerin.

> This is a formal role play – the *Sie* form will be used throughout.

1. Welchen Job Sie suchen

> Was für einen Job suchen Sie?

> Ich suche einen Job als Babysitterin.

> You need to respond to the precise details here.

2. Job – wann

> Wann wollen Sie arbeiten?

> Ich will im Sommer arbeiten.

> Here you need to say when you want to work (month, season, now).

3. !

> Wo arbeiten Sie im Moment?

> Im Restaurant.

> Check you know your question words in German – see page 106 of the Grammar section now to make sure.

Over to you!

2 Now look at the remaining two prompts below and make notes on how you would ask these questions. Then listen to the audio file before responding to all five prompts yourself.

4. ? Job – Grund
5. ? Lohn

Listen to the recording

Languages beyond the classroom

Working abroad

1   Read this report about Lenny's dream of working abroad.

> ● ● ●
>
> Mein Traum ist es, im Ausland zu arbeiten. Ich habe gute Noten in Englisch und ich lerne jetzt auch Französisch als zweite Fremdsprache. Ich will unbedingt um die Welt reisen, bevor ich zwanzig werde!
>
> Sprachen finde ich nicht schwierig, und die Grammatik interessiert mich besonders, weil ich logisch denke und keine Schwierigkeiten damit habe.
>
> Ich finde es schade, dass meine Freunde wenig Interesse an Fremdsprachen haben. Nach dem Abitur plane ich, als Freiwilliger ein Jahr in London zu verbringen. Ich kann dann meine Englischkenntnisse verbessern und Erfahrung für meinen Lebenslauf sammeln.

Put a cross [×] in the correct box.

(i)   Lenny is learning … language(s).

☐	**A** two
☐	**B** three
☐	**C** one
☐	**D** no

(1 mark)

> Train yourself to focus on the information in a text which is relevant to the question and look out for key words.

(ii)   Lenny is keen to …

☐	**A** work
☐	**B** travel
☐	**C** study
☐	**D** stay at home

(1 mark)

(iii) Lenny is … at learning languages.

☐	**A** unsuccessful
☐	**B** poor
☐	**C** slow
☐	**D** adept

(1 mark)

(iv) Lenny's friends … his attitude.

☐	**A** like
☐	**B** pity
☐	**C** ignore
☐	**D** share

(1 mark)

(v)   Lenny's plans will help him …

☐	**A** at school
☐	**B** improve himself
☐	**C** earn money
☐	**D** meet new people

(1 mark)

Volunteering

WRITING
Guided

Freiwillige Arbeit

1   Übersetze **ins Deutsche**.

> Last month I did voluntary work at the hospital.
> Although I enjoyed the work, I found the days very tiring.
> This year my brother is volunteering in an animal shelter.
> He would really like to work abroad to help animals that
> are suffering from diseases.

> Different verbs use different cases!
> Here, you might choose to use
> *arbeiten in* + dative, *gefallen* (to
> like) + dative, *finden* + accusative,
> *leiden unter* (to suffer from) + dative.

Letzten Monat habe ich freiwillige Arbeit im Krankenhaus gemacht. Obwohl

....

....

....

....

....

....

....

....

....

....

....

.... **(12 marks)**

> Adjectives agree and are in the accusative case for time
> expressions: *letztes Jahr, letzte Woche, letzten Monat*.

> The verb goes to the end of the clause after subordinating conjunctions such as *obwohl*.

LISTENING
TRACK 52

Listen to the recording

Freiwillige Arbeit

2   Du hörst einen Bericht im deutschen Schulradio über freiwillige Arbeit für die
Klasse elf.

Wie ist die Arbeit? Trag entweder **anstrengend**, **neu**, **einfach** oder **abwechslungsreich**
ein. Du kannst jedes Wort mehr als einmal verwenden.

(a)   Für jeden Schüler ist die Stellensuche immer .... **(1 mark)**

(b)   Das Schulverkehrsmittel ist .... **(1 mark)**

(c)   Das Programmangebot ist jedes Jahr .... **(1 mark)**

(d)   Die Schüler finden das Freiwilligenprogramm oft .... **(1 mark)**

(e)   Letztes Jahr war die Arbeit im Freien .... **(1 mark)**

Training

Ausbildungsangebote

1 Lies die Ausbildungsangebote.

● ○ ○

Büro	Sind Sie freundlich und teamfähig? Bei uns lernen Sie die nötigen Fähigkeiten, um Bürokaufmann/-frau zu werden. Durch diverse Aufgaben und schriftliche Prüfungen erhalten Sie wichtige professionelle Computerkenntnisse.
Kaufhaus	Hier bekommen Sie eine Top-Ausbildung mit Top-Gehalt und tollen Benefits. Jedes Jahr kommen 40 Lehrlinge zu uns, um eine wertvolle Ausbildung zu erhalten.
Restaurant	Bei uns lernen Sie die Geheimnisse der Gastronomie von innen kennen. Und dabei haben Sie immer Spaß an der Arbeit.
Supermarkt	Hier lernen Sie, wie man am besten mit Kunden und eventuell mit schwierigen Situationen an der Kasse umgeht.

Wo macht man das? Trag entweder **Büro**, **Kaufhaus**, **Restaurant** oder
Supermarkt ein. Du kannst jedes Wort mehr als einmal verwenden.

(a) Im .... hat man Kontakt mit Kunden. **(1 mark)**

(b) Im .... lernt man Tipps für die Küche. **(1 mark)**

(c) Im .... muss man ähnlich wie in der Schule weiter lernen. **(1 mark)**

(d) Im .... verdient man viel Geld. **(1 mark)**

> Look for money-related words in the text such as *Gehalt*.

(e) Im .... muss man gern mit anderen Leuten arbeiten. **(1 mark)**

Apprenticeships

2 Working at an Austrian training office, you receive these requests from Hannes about apprenticeships. Listen to the recording and answer the following questions **in English**.

Listen to the recording

(a) What does Hannes want to train as?

.... **(1 mark)**

(b) How is he getting experience?

.... **(1 mark)**

(c) What is he able to do for the customers?

.... **(1 mark)**

(d) What does he want to know about the position?

.... **(1 mark)**

> Don't be put off by speakers asking questions in a listening passage as well as making statements – if you read the questions on the exam paper before you listen, you can prepare yourself fully for what you are about to hear.

Part-time jobs

Meine Freunde

1   Lies Richards Blogeintrag.

> The pronoun *dieser* takes the same endings as *der* and means 'this', just as *jener* means 'that'.

● ● ●

Mina trägt jeden Tag Zeitungen aus, aber sie findet es echt schwer, weil sie so früh aufstehen muss. Warum macht sie also diesen Job? Sie braucht das Geld für den Sommerurlaub.

Samstags sieht man **Felix** bei der Arbeit in einem Supermarkt. Es macht ihm viel Spaß, aber die Arbeitszeiten sind lang. Das Beste ist, wenn er an der Kasse arbeiten darf, weil er sehr gern mit den Kunden spricht.

Mehmet hilft seinem Onkel, der ein türkisches Restaurant in der Stadtmitte besitzt. Dieses Wochenende darf er als Kellner im Speisesaal arbeiten und das findet er sehr interessant, obwohl die Kunden ihm manchmal auf die Nerven gehen.

Wähl die richtige Antwort [×].

(i)   Das Beste an Minas Job ist …

☐	**A** das Gehalt
☐	**B** der Chef
☐	**C** das Frühaufstehen
☐	**D** die Natur

(1 mark)

(ii)   Felix arbeitet …

☐	**A** am Sonntag
☐	**B** am Wochentag
☐	**C** am Wochenende
☐	**D** jeden Tag

(1 mark)

(iii)   Seine Lieblingsaufgabe hat mit … zu tun.

☐	**A** Mitarbeitern
☐	**B** Aufräumen
☐	**C** Essen
☐	**D** Geld

(1 mark)

(iv)   Mehmet arbeitet in der …

☐	**A** Türkei
☐	**B** Gastronomie
☐	**C** Schule
☐	**D** Kantine

(1 mark)

(v)   Mehmet findet … manchmal nervig.

☐	**A** das Publikum
☐	**B** den Onkel
☐	**C** die Speisekarte
☐	**D** die Mitarbeiter

(1 mark)

> *Mitarbeiter* is simply a 'colleague', i.e. somebody who works **with** you!

Work for teenagers

2   You hear a radio report with Frau Wyss advising teenagers about working. What does she say? Choose the **two** correct answers.

> Keep revising your numbers in German, so they don't trip you up in any of the exams.

Listen to the recording

> Just because you hear *acht Stunden*, it does not mean statement **C** is correct. Listen carefully to find out what *acht Stunden* is linked to. It is not hours a week!

A	All teenagers are regarded as children as far as work goes.	☐
B	You have to be 13 before you can have a paper round.	☐
C	15-year-olds can only work for 8 hours a week.	☐
D	Some teenagers are allowed to work at the weekends.	☐
E	Teenagers cannot work in the sports sector.	☐

(2 marks)

CV

Matching questions and answers

1 Match the student's replies (A–E) to the teacher's questions (1–5).

> Develop your Conversation by giving examples and reasons for your statements, as well as including a question to your teacher: *Ich mag Fußball* is accurate, but it does not make for a flowing conversation. A better way would be: *Seit meiner Kindheit spiele ich gern Fußball und eines Tages möchte ich Profifußballer werden. Wie finden Sie Fußball?*

1 Was sind deine Charaktereigenschaften?

A Seit zwei Jahren trage ich einmal pro Woche eine Lokalzeitung in der Gegend aus. Das finde ich ziemlich anstrengend, weil die meisten Leute im Hochhaus wohnen und ich die Treppen immer hinauf- und hinuntergehen muss, um die Zeitungen abzuliefern.

2 Was für Arbeitserfahrung hast du schon gesammelt?

B In zehn Jahren möchte ich einen gut bezahlten Job haben, bei dem ich in den Ferien viel reisen kann. Ich möchte am allerliebsten nach Amerika reisen, weil ich noch nie dort war und mir das Land sehr aufregend vorkommt.

3 Was wirst du nach den Prüfungen machen?

C Ich habe keine festen Pläne für die Arbeitswelt, aber ich meine, dass ich vielleicht Lehrer werden will, weil das ein guter Beruf ist. Natürlich werde ich zuerst auf die Uni gehen, um dafür qualifiziert zu sein.

4 Wo würdest du gern in Zukunft arbeiten?

D Ich bin selbstbewusst und freundlich, und ich finde, das sind wichtige Charaktereigenschaften, wenn man mit anderen Leuten arbeitet. Ich komme gut mit Leuten aus, weil ich tolerant und nicht egoistisch bin.

> Don't forget conjunctions to help your sentences flow: *und* and *aber* are very easy to slip in, and they do not change the word order.

5 Was für einen Lebensstil möchtest du in zehn Jahren haben?

E Diesen Sommer werde ich nach den Prüfungen Kurzurlaub machen, bevor ich im September in die Oberstufe gehe, um mit der Schule weiterzumachen. Ich werde Naturwissenschaften und Deutsch wählen, weil diese meine Lieblingsfächer sind.

1 D   3 ………   5 ………

2 ………   4 ………

Global sports events

Weltmeisterschaften

1   Look at the photo and read the task. Then fill in the gaps in the three sample answers with the missing verbs.
This will give you practice in completing the writing activity in the exam – where you will have to write your entire answer. You can practise the whole task in Question 2.

Du bist bei einem Sportevent. Du postest dieses Foto online für deine Freunde.

Beschreib das Foto **und** schreib deine Meinung über globale Sportevents.

Schreib ungefähr 20–30 Wörter **auf Deutsch**.

(a) Ich .... mit meinen Freunden bei einem Fußballspiel.

Das Wetter .... sonnig und warm, und es

.... viel Lärm. Ich .... Sportevents

sehr stressig, und ich .... sie mir lieber im Fernsehen an.

> ist
> sehe
> bin
> gibt
> finde

(b) Wir .... bei der Fußballmeisterschaft.

Das .... mir Spaß, weil ich ein großer Fußballfan

.... Sportevents .... ich immer

sehr spannend, aber diese Eintrittskarte .... wirklich

zu teuer.

> finde
> sind
> macht
> bin
> ist

(c) Wir............................... uns ein Fußballspiel an. Die Stimmung

im Stadion............................... wunderbar und die Fußballer

.... sehr begabt. Ich...............................

solche Events, weil die Sportler mich............................... .

> liebe
> sehen
> inspirieren
> ist
> sind

> Make sure you are confident with present tense verb forms to tackle this activity – check on page 95 of the Grammar section for the endings with all the pronouns. Make sure you also learn the key irregular verbs *haben* (to have) and *sein* (to be).

My photo message

2   Now complete the task above for yourself on a separate piece of paper, using the sample answers to help you.

> Always check your writing at the end – does each verb match the person: e.g. *ich bin* **but** *wir sind*?

Global music events

Globale Musikevents

1 Read the extended writing task and write down some key words you consider useful to use in response to each bullet point.

Du willst, dass ein globales Musikevent in deiner Stadt stattfindet.

Schreib einen Brief an deinen Freund.

Du **musst** über diese Punkte schreiben:

- **welches Musikevent du gesehen hast**

- **ein erfolgreiches Musikevent letztes Jahr**

- **Vorteile des Events für deine Stadt**

- **warum das Event gut für die Stadt wäre.**

Rechtfertige deine Ideen und Meinungen. Schreib ungefähr 130–150 Wörter **auf Deutsch**.

> Don't jeopardise the accuracy of your writing by being over-ambitious. In the exam, stick to structures you are familiar with. Learning a good range of idioms and constructions before the exam is key to doing well in this kind of task.

> Read the introduction to the task carefully and start focusing on just that: key words are *globales Musikevent* and *in deiner Stadt*.

> You can mention type of music, location, facilities, time of year …

> You need to describe the event in the past tense here.

> Use the future tense as you consider what **advantages** the music event **will** bring to your town.

> Now you need the subjunctive: remember the shortened forms *könnte* (could), *wäre* (would be) and *hätte* to support your writing here.

> Make sure you learn a stock of expressions to carry out this part of the task: *Meiner Meinung nach … , Ich meine, dass … . Das Beste wäre … , Im Großen und Ganzen …*

Sample writing

Guided

2 Read this student's answer to the task and put the paragraphs in the correct order to match the bullet points above. Then prepare your own answer to this task on a separate page.

(a) Mit dem Einkommen aus dem Event könnten wir in Zukunft eine neue Konzerthalle bauen oder auch Jugendaktivitäten in jedem Stadtteil verbessern. Wir könnten zum Beispiel ein Orchester gründen und unseren jungen Leuten musikalische Angebote machen.

(b) Wenn wir jetzt ein Event hier organisieren, werden Leute aus der ganzen Welt hierher kommen und Geld in unseren Geschäften und Restaurants ausgeben. Die Stadt wird reicher werden und auch berühmt.

(c) Ein globales Musikfest in unserer Stadt ist eine tolle Gelegenheit, die besten internationalen Bands in unsere Stadt einzuladen, finde ich.

(d) Letzten Sommer habe ich zum ersten Mal ein Musikevent besucht, wo ich zwei Tage im Zelt übernachtet und viele nette Leute kennengelernt habe. Das war ein einmaliges Erlebnis, weil die Musik spitze war, aber leider musste ich ziemlich weit mit der Bahn fahren, um dorthin zu kommen.

Correct order:

1   c   2 ………   3 ………   4 ………

> Get your *ei* and *ie* the right way round! If you pronounce the word as in English 'my', spell it *ei*: *arbeiten*, **Ei**nkommen; if you pronounce the word as in English 'me', write it *ie*: **die**, *viele*.

Being green

Die Umwelt

> Learn your time words: *ab und zu* (now and again), *manchmal* (sometimes), *immer* (always), *nie* (never).

1   Übersetze **ins Deutsche**.

> Guided

(a) I always recycle bottles.

> If you are translating present tense verbs in the 'I' form, they mostly end in -e: *ich gehe, fahre, esse* …

Ich ....

.... **(2 marks)**

> Guided

(b) I never travel by bike.

Ich .... **(2 marks)**

(c) My parents always wear jumpers in the house.

> Always place the verb in the second position in a sentence.

....

.... **(2 marks)**

(d) Yesterday my friend Sara separated the rubbish.

....

....

.... **(3 marks)**

(e) She had a shower, because that is good for the environment.

> Use the adjective for 'environmentally friendly' here – it conveys the same meaning and is a straightforward way to translate this.

....

....

.... **(3 marks)**

Green family

2   You hear an interview with Herr Birnenstock, who blogs about his family's eco activities.

Listen to the interview and answer the following questions **in English**. You do not need to write in full sentences.

Listen to the recording

(a) Why did Herr Birnenstock start his blog?

.... **(1 mark)**

(b) Give **one** example of how the family helps the environment on a daily basis.

.... **(1 mark)**

(c) How does Frau Birnenstock use her photography skills to help raise awareness?

.... **(1 mark)**

(d) Give **one** detail of what the daughter blogs about.

.... **(1 mark)**

(e) Give **one** detail of what the son blogs about.

.... **(1 mark)**

Protecting the environment

READING

Guided

Translation

1 Translate this passage **into English**.

> Die Luftverschmutzung in meiner Stadt ist schrecklich, besonders wenn das Wetter sehr heiß ist. Der Flughafen befindet sich nur fünf Kilometer von unserer Wohnung entfernt, und die Autobahn ist auch ganz nah. Wir sollten alle die Umwelt schützen und öfter die öffentlichen Verkehrsmittel benutzen, anstatt mit dem Auto zu fahren.

Break words down to discover if they are two or more smaller words joined together: *Luft* (air) + *Verschmutzung* (pollution) = 'air pollution'.

The expression *X Kilometer entfernt* translates as 'X kilometres away'.

The air pollution in my town is dreadful, especially when the weather is very hot. The airport ....

....

....

....

....

....

....

....

....

....

....   **(7 marks)**

LISTENING
TRACK 56

Eco club

2 What do these people do to help the environment?

Listen to the recording and put a cross [x] in each one of the **three** correct boxes.

Listen to the recording

A	I work there every day.	☐
B	I read about the rainforest.	☐
C	We protect plant species.	☐
D	We look after small creatures.	☐
E	I eat organic food.	☐
F	We recycle food.	☐
G	I collect bottles.	☐

(3 marks)

WRITING

Even if you are a Higher tier student, don't ignore the Foundation activities in this Workbook. They are a useful way of checking you really are familiar with the topics.

Natural resources

Eine Öko-Zynikerin findet ihr Grünes Gewissen und die große Liebe by
Vanessa Farquharson, translated by Gerlinde Schermer-Rauwolf und Robert A. Weiß

1 Read the extract from the text.

The author is worried about the environment.

> Ich war von CO₂-Gewissensbissen geplagt, weil ich an diesem Tag allein mit dem Auto – nicht mit der **Fahrgemeinschaft** – zur Arbeit und zurück gefahren war.
>
> Ich dachte über den Kreis des Zynismus und den Kreis der Hoffnung nach, worüber ich gerade im Handbuch für eine bessere Welt gelesen hatte.
>
> 1. Man stößt auf ein Problem
> 2. möchte etwas **dagegen** tun
> 3. weiß nicht, wie
> 4. tut also gar nichts
> 5. ist deprimiert und verärgert, fühlt sich machtlos
> 6. kommt zu dem Schluss, dass man nichts tun kann
> 7. beginnt, sich zu verschließen
> 8. will immer weniger von Problemen wissen.

> **Fahrgemeinschaft:** Use your knowledge of the verb *fahren* (to drive) and *Gemeinschaft* (society) to work out what this means.

> **dagegen:** The preposition *gegen* means 'against' and *dagegen* just means 'against it'.

Put a cross [×] in the correct box.

(i)   The author is having difficulty …

☐	**A** relaxing
☐	**B** reading
☐	**C** dancing
☐	**D** balancing

(1 mark)

(ii) When the author goes to work she usually …

☐	**A** goes on foot
☐	**B** cycles
☐	**C** drives alone
☐	**D** shares lifts

(1 mark)

(iii) The author has read about …

☐	**A** decorating her home
☐	**B** travelling the world
☐	**C** improving the world
☐	**D** writing books

(1 mark)

(iv) The effect cynical people have on environmental problems is …

☐	**A** an improvement
☐	**B** zero
☐	**C** a solution
☐	**D** huge

(1 mark)

(v)   A cynical person might feel …

☐	**A** helpless
☐	**B** powerful
☐	**C** satisfied
☐	**D** content

(1 mark)

Campaigns

Campaigns

1 Look at the photo and draw lines to match the questions with the correct answers.

1	Wer ist im Bild?	**A**	Das Mädchen auf der linken Seite schreibt.
2	Wo sind sie?	**B**	Es gibt vier Personen im Bild.
3	Was machen sie?	**C**	Die Teenager sehen glücklich aus und lächeln.
4	Was sieht man links?	**D**	Sie arbeiten freiwillig, denke ich.
5	Wie sehen die jungen Leute aus?	**E**	Sie sind wahrscheinlich in einem Raum, wo man Lebensmittel und Kleidung sortiert.

My photo description

2 Now look at the picture-based task for the photo and read this student's answers to the second bullet point. Then prepare your own answers to the remaining three bullet points.

Schau dir das Foto an und sei bereit, über Folgendes zu sprechen:

- **Beschreibung des Fotos**
- **Deine Meinung zu Spendenaktionen für andere**

Mir ist es wichtig, Spendenaktionen für andere zu machen, weil zum Beispiel viele Familien in Armut leben. An unserer Schule haben wir oft Spendenaktionen und ich finde das toll. Zum Beispiel sammeln wir Lebensmittel und Kleidung für Menschen in unserer Stadt oder wir backen und verkaufen Kuchen und Kekse in der Pause. Jede Klasse macht eine Spendenaktion und dann geben wir alles einer Organisation.

> Your first task is to **describe** the photo in as much detail as you can: include colours, sizes, objects, people, clothes, weather … anything you can **see**!

> Have a good stock of adjectives to express your opinions: *gut, wichtig, schlecht, nutzlos …*

- **Wie du anderen geholfen hast**

> Past tense here – but keep it simple. Best to stick to structures you know and deliver your answers accurately and clearly.

- **Wie man am besten anderen helfen kann**

> This next bullet point includes a modal construction. Make sure you use this in your answer: *kann … machen.*

- **Deine Meinung zum Tierschutz**

> Start your final opinion with a phrase, such as *Ich finde, Ich glaube, Ich meine, Meiner Meinung nach ist …* If you want to use a clause with *dass*, remember to put the verb at the end: *Ich finde, dass Aktionen für Tiere (gut/schrecklich) sind.*

3 Look at the Answers section on page 127 to read and listen to the student's answers to the task in full.

Good causes

Katastrophen

1   Lies Katjas Blogeintrag.

> Am liebsten nehme ich an einer gesponserten Schweigestunde in der Klasse teil. Das macht immer Spaß, weil es die Lehrer echt ärgert, wenn man ihre Fragen nicht beantworten kann.
>
> Diese Woche backe ich jeden Abend Kuchen zu Hause, um sie am folgenden Tag in der Aula zu verkaufen. Wir sammeln Geld für die Katastrophe in Asien.
>
> Ich sehe mir die Bilder im Internet an, und ich finde es schockierend, dass die Überschwemmungen alles zerstört haben. Diese Familien müssen jetzt im Zelt wohnen.
>
> Mir ist es wichtig, Geld für solche Katastrophen zu sammeln. Habt ihr auch Vorschläge?

Highlight any words you do **not** understand on your first reading. After you have completed the task and read the text through a couple of times, how many do you still not understand? Do you need to understand them to complete the task?

Füll die Lücke in jedem Satz mit einem Wort aus dem Kasten.
Es gibt mehr Wörter als Lücken.

> Currywurst   Ideen   Keine   Bibliothek   Geld   online
>
> egoistisch   nichts   Manche   Gebäck   Schule

(a)   Sie nimmt gern an Aktionen in der .... teil.   **(1 mark)**

(b)   Katja bereitet abends .... vor.   **(1 mark)**

(c)   Katja lernt .... über die Katastrophe.   **(1 mark)**

(d)   .... der Überlebenden schlafen in Gebäuden.   **(1 mark)**

(e)   Katja bittet um ....   **(1 mark)**

Charity giving

2   Your German exchange partner is talking about how her friends regard charity giving. What does she say about them? Listen to the recording and put a cross [×] in each one of the **three** correct boxes.

Listen to the recording

A	supports children	☐
B	keeps money for self	☐
C	raises lots of money	☐
D	helps out rather than raises money	☐
E	does sponsored events	☐
F	gives own money away	☐
G	bakes sweet things to sell	☐

(3 marks)

> Make sure you have completed as many task-types as possible in this Workbook across all **five** of the topic areas – they will probably all come up somewhere in the exams.

Gender and plurals

> In the nominative, German nouns are either *der* (masculine), *die* (feminine) or *das* (neuter).
>
> *der / die / das* = the
>
> **der** Hund   **die** Katze   **das** Kaninchen

1 Put a circle round the correct article.

(a) der / die / das Abfalleimer (*m.*)

(b) der / die / das Kino (*n.*)

(c) der / die / das Krankenschwester (*f.*)

(d) der / die / das Rucksack (*m.*)

(e) der / die / das Handy (*n.*)

(f) der / die / das Restaurant (*n.*)

(g) der / die / das Autobahn (*f.*)

(h) der / die / das Sportlehrer (*m.*)

(i) der / die / das Umwelt (*f.*)

2 Complete with *der*, *die* or *das*.

(a) .... Haus ist modern. (*n.*)

(b) .... Schüler heißt Max. (*m.*)

(c) .... Schülerin heißt Demet. (*f.*)

(d) .... Computer ist kaputt. (*m.*)

(e) .... Zug fährt langsam. (*m.*)

(f) .... Bank ist geschlossen. (*f.*)

(g) .... Zeitung kostet 1 Euro. (*f.*)

(h) .... Buch ist langweilig. (*n.*)

> In the accusative, the article *der* changes to *den* (masculine), but *die* and *das* don't change.
>
> | | *m.* | *f.* | *n.* | *pl.* |
> |------------|------|------|------|-------|
> | **Accusative** | **den** | die | das | die |
>
> Wir mögen **den** Sportlehrer.

3 Write in *den*, *die* or *das*.

(a) Wir haben .... Pizza gegessen. (*f.*)

(b) Wir können .... Krankenhaus sehen. (*n.*)

(c) Ich mache .... Hausaufgabe. (*f.*)

(d) Vati kauft .... Pullover. (*m.*)

(e) Liest du .... Buch? (*n.*)

(f) Ich wasche .... Wagen. (*m.*)

> German plurals come in many forms. The most common ones are *–e* and *–n*, but many are irregular, maybe adding an umlaut or simply staying the same.
>
> (S) Brief   ⟶   (P) Brief**e**
> (S) Tasse   ⟶   (P) Tasse**n**
> (S) Teller ⟶   (P) Teller
> (S) Glas   ⟶   (P) Gl**ä**s**er**

4 Write **S** if the noun is singular and **P** if it is plural. If it could be either, put **E**.

Haus .... , Buch .... , Männer .... , Autos .... , Häuser .... , Supermarkt .... ,

Tisch .... , Mann .... , Supermärkte .... , Tische .... , Handys .... ,

Zimmer .... , Bilder .... , Computer ....

Cases and prepositions

The prepositions which trigger a change to the accusative are: *bis, entlang* (after the noun), *für, gegen, ohne* and *um*.

	m.	f.	n.	pl.
Nominative	der	die	das	die
Accusative	de**n**	die	das	die
Nominative	ein	eine	ein	keine
Accusative	eine**n**	eine	ein	keine

1 Write in *den, die, das, einen, eine* or *ein*.

    (a) um .... Ecke (*round the corner*) (*f.*)

    (b) durch .... Stadt (*through the town*) (*f.*)

    (c) ohne .... Auto (*without a car*) (*n.*)

    (d) für .... Schule (*for the school*) (*f.*)

    (e) für .... Freund (*for a friend*) (*m.*)

    (f) gegen .... Wand (*against the wall*) (*f.*)

    (g) bis .... Wald (*up to a wood*) (*m.*)

    (h) .... Straße entlang (*along the road*) (*f.*)

The prepositions which trigger a change to the dative are: *aus, außer, bei, gegenüber, mit, nach, seit, von* and *zu*.

	m.	f.	n.	pl.
Nominative	der	die	das	die
Dative	de**m**	de**r**	de**m**	de**n**
Nominative	ein	eine	ein	keine
Dative	eine**m**	eine**r**	eine**m**	keine**n**

2 Write in *dem, der, einem* or *einer*.

    (a) mit .... Bus (*by bus*) (*m.*)

    (b) seit .... Sommer (*since the summer*) (*m.*)

    (c) zu .... Bank (*to the bank*) (*f.*)

    (d) nach .... Party (*after the party*) (*f.*)

    (e) bei .... Freund (*at a friend's house*) (*m.*)

    (f) von .... Onkel (*from an uncle*) (*m.*)

    (g) gegenüber .... Tankstelle (*opposite the petrol station*) (*f.*)

    (h) außer .... Lehrerin (*apart from the teacher*) (*f.*)

    (i) aus .... Raum (*out of the room*) (*m.*)

A few prepositions trigger a change to the genitive: *trotz, wegen* and *während*

	m.	f.	n.	pl.
Nominative	der	die	das	die
Genitive	de**s**	de**r**	de**s**	de**r**
Nominative	ein	eine	ein	keine
Genitive	eine**s**	eine**r**	eine**s**	keine**r**

3 Write in *der* or *des*.

    (a) wegen .... Wetters (*because of the weather*) (*n.*)

    (b) während .... Stunde (*during the lesson*) (*f.*)

    (c) trotz .... Regens (*despite the rain*) (*m.*)

Dative and accusative prepositions

These prepositions trigger a change to the accusative if there is **movement towards** a place, or the dative if there is **no movement**:

an (on, at)	*auf* (on)	*hinter* (behind)
in (in)	*neben* (next to)	*über* (over, above)
unter (under)	*vor* (in front of)	*zwischen* (between)

See page 86 for the accusative and dative forms of articles.

1 Circle the correct article.

(a) Wir fahren in **der / die** Stadt. (*f.*)

(b) Meine Schwester ist in **der / die** Schule. (*f.*)

(c) Das Essen steht auf **den / dem** Tisch. (*m.*)

(d) Ich steige auf **die / der** Mauer. (*f.*)

(e) Wir hängen das Bild an **der / die** Wand. (*f.*)

(f) Jetzt ist das Bild an **der / die** Wand. (*f.*)

(g) Die Katze läuft hinter **einen / einem** Schrank. (*m.*)

(h) Wo ist die Katze jetzt? Hinter **den / dem** Schrank. (*m.*)

(i) Die Bäckerei steht zwischen **einem / einen** Supermarkt (*m.*) und **einer / eine** Post. (*f.*)

(j) Das Flugzeug fliegt über **die / der** Stadt. (*f.*)

(k) Ich stelle die Flaschen in **dem / den** Schrank. (*m.*)

(l) Der Bus steht an **der / die** Haltestelle. (*f.*)

Some verbs work with a preposition which is followed by the accusative.

2 Circle the correct article. Then translate the sentences into English.

(a) Die Kinder streiten sich über **das / dem** Fernsehprogramm. (*n.*)

....

(b) Wir freuen uns auf **das / dem** Fest. (*n.*)

....

(c) Ich ärgere mich oft über **der / die** Arbeit. (*f.*)

....

(d) Martin hat sich an **der / die** Sonne gewöhnt. (*f.*)

....

(e) Wie lange warten Sie auf **der / die** Straßenbahn? (*f.*)

....

Certain special phrases have a preposition followed by either the accusative or the dative.
You have to learn these.

3 Draw lines to link the German and English phrases.

1 auf dem Land   A *on the internet*

2 vor allem   B *on the right*

3 auf die Nerven   C *in the country*

4 auf der rechten Seite   D *on (someone's) nerves*

5 im Internet   E *above all*

Dieser / jeder, kein / mein

Dieser (this) and *jener* (that) follow the pattern of *der, die, das*.

	m.	*f.*	*n.*	*pl.*
Nominative	dieser	diese	dieses	diese
Accusative	diesen	diese	dieses	diese
Dative	diesem	dieser	diesem	diesen

1   Add the endings.

    (a)   *this man*   dies.........Mann (*m.*)

    (b)   *with this man*   mit dies.........Mann (*m.*)

    (c)   *this woman*   dies.........Frau (*f.*)

    (d)   *for this woman*   für dies.........Frau (*f.*)

    (e)   *that animal*   jen.........Tier (*n.*)

    (f)   *on that animal*   auf jen.........Tier (*n.*)

Kein, mein, dein, sein, ihr, unser, euer (eure) and *Ihr* follow the pattern of *ein*.

	m.	*f.*	*n.*	*pl.*
Nominative	kein	keine	kein	keine
Accusative	keinen	keine	kein	keine
Dative	keinem	keiner	keinem	keinen

2   Complete the words where necessary with the correct ending.

    (a)   Unser.........Schwester heißt Monika. (*f.*)

    (b)   Ich habe kein.........Bruder. (*m.*)

    (c)   Mein.........Schule ist nicht sehr groß. (*f.*)

    (d)   Hast du dein.........Laptop vergessen? (*m.*)

    (e)   Wie ist Ihr.........Name, bitte? (*m.*)

    (f)   Meine Lehrerin hat ihr.........Schulbücher nicht mit. (*pl.*)

    (g)   Wo steht Ihr.........Auto? (*n.*)

    (h)   Wir arbeiten in unser.........Büro. (*n.*)

    (i)   Wo ist euer.........Wohnung? (*f.*)

    (j)   Mein.........Lieblingsfächer sind Mathe und Informatik. (*pl.*)

    (k)   Wie heißt dein.........Freundin? (*f.*)

    (l)   Leider haben wir kein.........Zeit. (*f.*)

    (m)   Ihr.........E-Mail war nicht sehr höflich. (*f.*)

    (n)   Olaf geht mit sein.........Freund spazieren. (*m.*)

    (o)   Adele singt ihr.........besten Hits. (*pl.*)

    (p)   Wo habt ihr euer.........Auto stehen lassen? (*n.*)

'Specials'

    (q)   Ich habe ....Ahnung. (*I've no idea.*) (*f.*)

    (r)   Ich habe ....Lust. (*I don't want to.*) (*f.*)

    (s)   Das war ....Fehler. (*That was my mistake.*) (*m.*)

    (t)   ....Meinung nach ... (*In my opinion...*) (*f.*)

Had a go ☐   **Nearly there** ☐   **Nailed it!** ☐

Adjective endings

Adjectives after the definite article end in either *–e* or *–en*.

	m.	*f.*	*n.*	*pl.*
Nominative	der kleine Hund	die kleine Maus	das kleine Haus	die kleinen Kinder
Accusative	den kleinen Hund	die kleine Maus	das kleine Haus	die kleinen Kinder
Dative	dem kleinen Hund	der kleinen Maus	dem kleinen Haus	den kleinen Kindern

1   Fill the gaps with the suggested adjective and its correct ending.

    (a)   Die .... Schülerin bekommt gute Noten. (*f.*, intelligent—)

    (b)   Wir fahren mit dem .... Bus in die Stadt. (*m.*, nächst—)

    (c)   Hast du den .... Vogel gesehen? (*m.*, gelb—)

    (d)   Der .... Lehrer ist streng. (*m.*, altmodisch—)

    (e)   Ich kaufe dieses .... Kleid. (*n.*, schwarz—)

    (f)   Die .... Reihenhäuser sind schön. (*pl.*, neugebaut—)

    (g)   Heute gehen wir in den .... Freizeitpark. (*m.*, modern—)

    (h)   Wir müssen dieses .... Fahrrad sauber machen. (*n.*, schmutzig—)

    (i)   Morgen gehen wir ins .... Einkaufszentrum. (*n.*, neu—)

    (j)   Der .... Zug kommt um 1 Uhr an. (*m.*, verspätet—)

Adjectives after the indefinite article have various endings. This also applies to *kein*, *mein*, *sein*, etc.

	m.	*f.*	*n.*	*pl.*
Nominative	ein kleiner Hund	eine kleine Maus	ein kleines Haus	meine kleinen Kinder
Accusative	einen kleinen Hund	eine kleine Maus	ein kleines Haus	meine kleinen Kinder
Dative	einem kleinen Hund	einer kleinen Maus	einem kleinen Haus	meinen kleinen Kindern

2   Fill the gaps with the suggested adjective and its correct ending.

    (a)   München ist eine .... Stadt. (*f.*, umweltfreundlich—)

    (b)   Ich suche ein .... T-Shirt. (*n.*, preiswert—)

    (c)   Marta hat ihre .... Handtasche verloren. (*f.*, modisch—)

    (d)   Wir haben unsere .... Hausaufgaben nicht gemacht. (*pl.*, schwierig—)

    (e)   Ich habe ein .... Bett gekauft. (*n.*, bequem—)

    (f)   Das ist ein .... Problem. (*n.*, groß—)

    (g)   Das war vielleicht eine .... Stunde! (*f.*, langweilig—)

    (h)   Diese .... Leute haben das Spiel verdorben. (*pl.*, idiotisch—)

    (i)   Mein Vater hat einen .... Unfall gehabt. (*m.*, schwer—)

    (j)   Klaus liebt seine .... Freundin. (*f.*, neu—)

    (k)   Wir haben kein .... Obst. (*n.*, frisch—)

    (l)   Maria hat einen .... Mantel gekauft. (*m.*, grün—)

Comparisons

To make comparisons between things, you use the comparative or superlative.

Add –er for the comparative, or add –(e)ste for the superlative.

Adjective: langsam – langsamer – langsamst- + ending (*slow, slower, slowest*)

Adverb: langsam – langsamer – am langsamsten (*slowly, more slowly, most slowly*)

1 Insert the comparative and superlative forms.

(a) Mathe ist langweilig, Physik ist ...., aber das ....
Fach ist Kunst.

(b) Oliver läuft schnell, Ali läuft ...., aber Tim läuft am
....

(c) Berlin ist schön, Paris ist ...., aber Wien ist
die .... Stadt.

(d) Rihanna ist cool, Katy Perry ist ...., aber Taylor Swift
ist die .... Sängerin.

(e) Metallica ist .... als Motörhead. (laut)

(f) Bremen ist .... als Hamburg. (klein)

(g) Deine Noten sind schlecht, aber meine sind noch ....

(h) Ich finde Englisch .... als Französisch, aber Deutsch finde ich am
.... (einfach)

(i) Skifahren ist .... als Radfahren. (schwierig)

(j) Mein Auto ist .... als dein Auto, aber das Auto meines Vaters ist am
.... (billig)

Some adjectives have small changes to the comparative and superlative forms.

2 Fill in the gaps with the words provided below, then translate the sentences into English.

beste / länger / höher / besser / größer / jünger / am längsten

(a) Ich bin .... als du. (jung)

....

(b) Die Alpen sind .... als der Snowdon. (hoch)

....

(c) München ist .... als Bonn. (groß)

....

(d) Meine Haare sind lang, Timos Haare sind ...., aber deine Haare sind
....

....

(e) Fußball ist gut, Handball ist ...., aber Tennis ist das
.... Spiel.

....

3 Compare your likes and dislikes by using *gern*, *lieber* and *am liebsten*.

(a) Ich spiele .... Basketball. (*like*)

(b) Ich esse .... Gemüse als Fleisch. (*prefer*)

(c) Am .... gehe ich schwimmen. (*like best*)

Personal pronouns

> Like *der*, *die* and *das*, pronouns change depending on what case they are in: nominative, accusative or dative.
>
> | Nominative | Accusative | Dative |
> |---|---|---|
> | ich | mich | mir |
> | du | dich | dir |
> | er | ihn | ihm |
> | sie | sie | ihr |
> | es | es | ihm |
> | wir | uns | uns |
> | ihr | euch | euch |
> | Sie/sie | Sie/sie | Ihnen/ihnen |

1   Use the correct pronoun in the appropriate case.

(a)   Ich liebe .... (*you, familiar*)

(b)   Liebst du .... ? (*me*)

(c)   Kommst du mit .... ? (*me*)

(d)   Mein Bruder ist nett. Ich mag .... gern. (*him*)

(e)   Ich habe keine Kreditkarte. Ich habe .... verloren. (*it*)

(f)   Ein Geschenk für .... ? Danke! (*us*)

(g)   Wir haben .... gestern gesehen. (*you, plural, familiar*)

(h)   Haben .... gut geschlafen? (*you, formal*)

(i)   Die Party ist bei .... (*me*)

(j)   Rolf hatte Hunger. Ich bin mit .... essen gegangen. (*him*)

(k)   Vergiss .... nicht! (*me*)

(l)   Wie heißt .... ? (*you, familiar*)

(m) Wie heißen .... ? (*you, formal*)

(n)   Meine Schwester ist krank. Gestern sind wir zu .... gegangen. (*her*)

> Certain special phrases use a dative pronoun.
>
> | | |
> |---|---|
> | es tut **mir** leid | *I am sorry* |
> | es gefällt **ihm** | *he likes it* |
> | es fällt **mir** schwer | *I find it difficult* |
> | es gelingt **mir** | *I succeed* |
> | es geht **mir** gut | *I'm well* |
> | es tut **ihr** weh | *it hurts her* |
> | das schmeckt **mir** | *that tastes good* |
> | das ist **mir** egal | *it's all the same to me* |

2   Fill in the gaps.

(a)   Schwimmen .... mir .... (= *I find it hard*)

(b)   Mmmm, Eis! .... es .... ? (= *do you [familiar] like the taste?/do you like it?*)

(c)   Aua! Das .... weh! (= *it hurts me*)

(d)   Leider .... es .... nicht gut. (= *we aren't well*)

(e)   Wer gewinnt im Fußball? Das ....
(= *I don't care*)

(f)   Es .... leid. (= *we are sorry*)

Word order

> In German sentences, the **second** item is always the **verb**. In the perfect tense, the part of *haben* or *sein* comes in second position (see below).
>
> Daniel **fährt** in die Stadt.
>
> Morgen **fährt** Daniel in die Stadt.

1 Rewrite these sentences with the new beginnings.

  (a) Die Fernsehsendung beginnt.

     Um 6 Uhr ....

  (b) Ich fahre mit dem Bus zur Arbeit.

     Jeden Tag ....

  (c) Meine Eltern sind krank.

     Leider ....

  (d) Man darf nicht rauchen.

     Hier ....

> In the perfect tense, the part of *haben* or *sein* comes in second position.
>
> Ich **bin** zum Jugendklub gegangen.
>
> Am Samstag **bin** ich zum Jugendklub gegangen.

2 Now rewrite these sentences.

  (a) Wir haben Eis gegessen.

     Gestern ....

  (b) Timo ist ins Kino gegangen.

     Manchmal...

  (c) Ali ist nach Frankreich gefahren.

     Letztes Jahr ....

  (d) Du hast Pommes gekauft.

     Heute Morgen ....

> Remember the word order in German: first **time**, then **manner**, then **place**.
>
>   T   M   P
>
> Ich spiele <u>jeden Tag</u> <u>mit meinem Bruder</u> <u>im Garten</u>.

3 Write out these sentences in the right order.

  (a) jeden Tag / Ich fahre / zur Schule / mit dem Rad

     ....

  (b) am Wochenende / Gehst du / zum Schwimmbad? / mit mir

     ....

  (c) oft / fern / Wir sehen / im Wohnzimmer

     ....

  (d) Tischtennis / Mehmet spielt / im Jugendklub / abends

     ....

  (e) im Büro / Mein Vater arbeitet / fleißig / seit 20 Jahren

     ....

  (f) heute Abend / Willst du / Pizza essen? / im Restaurant / mit mir

     ....

Had a go ☐   Nearly there ☐   Nailed it! ☐

Conjunctions

> The most common conjunction that introduces a subordinate clause is *weil* (because). It sends the verb to the end.
>
> Ich gehe oft auf Partys, **weil** sie lustig sind.

1 Join these sentences together using *weil*. Write the sentences out.

(a) Claudia will Sportlehrerin werden. Sie ist sportlich.

....

(b) Ich kann dich nicht anrufen. Mein Handy funktioniert nicht.

....

(c) Wir fahren nach Spanien. Das Wetter ist dort so schön.

....

(d) Du darfst nicht im Garten spielen. Es regnet noch.

....

(e) Peter hat seine Hausaufgaben nicht gemacht. Er ist faul.

....

(f) Ich mag Computerspiele. Sie sind so aufregend.

....

> The following conjunctions also send the verb to the end: *als, bevor, bis, da, damit, dass, nachdem, ob, obwohl, während, was, wie, wenn*. In the perfect tense, the part of *haben* or *sein* comes last. In the future tense, it is *werden* that comes at the end.
>
> Ich habe Golf gespielt, **während** du eingekauft **hast**.

2 Join the sentences together using the conjunction indicated. Write the sentences out.

(a) Du kannst abwaschen. Ich koche. (während)

....

(b) Wir kaufen oft ein. Wir sind in der Stadt. (wenn)

....

(c) Ich kann nicht zur Party kommen. Ich werde arbeiten. (da)

....

(d) Lasst uns früh aufstehen. Wir können wandern. (damit)

....

(e) Meine Eltern waren böse. Ich bin nicht spät nach Hause gekommen. (obwohl)

....

(f) Ich habe es nicht gewusst. Du bist krank. (dass)

....

(g) Papa hat geraucht. Er war jung. (als)

....

(h) Ich weiß nicht. Man repariert einen Computer. (wie)

....

(i) Wir können schwimmen gehen. Das Wetter ist gut. (wenn)

....

(j) Wir müssen warten. Es regnet nicht mehr. (bis)

....

More on word order

> *um … zu* means 'in order to'. It needs an infinitive at the end of the clause.
>
> Wir gehen in den Park, **um** Tennis **zu** spielen.

1 Combine these sentences with *um … zu*.

(a) Wir fahren in die Stadt. Wir kaufen Lebensmittel.

....

(b) Viele Leute spielen Tennis. Sie werden fit.

....

(c) Boris spart Geld. Er kauft ein Motorrad.

....

(d) Meine Schwester geht zur Abendschule. Sie lernt Französisch.

....

(e) Ich bin gestern zum Imbiss gegangen. Ich esse gern Pommes.

....

> There are some other expressions which use *zu* in the same way.

2 Complete the sentences.

(a) Das Orchester beginnt .... (*to play*)

(b) Wir hoffen, ... (*to learn Spanish*)

(c) Oliver versucht, ... (*to play guitar*)

> Relative pronouns, *der*, *die* or *das* (expressing 'who' or 'that' or 'which'), send the verb to the end of the clause.
>
> das Mädchen, das krank ist   *the girl who is ill*

3 Translate these expressions into German. You will find the expressions jumbled up in the box below.

(a) the girl who plays tennis

....

(b) the boy who sings well

....

(c) the man who speaks German

....

(d) the house (*n.*) that is old

....

(e) the subject (*n.*) that is hard

....

(f) the car (*n.*) that is broken

....

(g) the cup (*f.*) that is full

....

das Auto,	das Fach,	der Deutsch spricht	das alt ist
der Junge,	das Mädchen,	das kaputt ist	das schwer ist
der Mann,	das Haus,	der gut singt	die voll ist
die Tasse,			das Tennis spielt

The present tense

Verb endings in the present tense change according to who or what is doing the action.

ich	mach**e**	*I do/make*
du	mach**st**	*you do/make*
er/sie/es/man	mach**t**	*he/she/it/one does/makes*
wir	mach**en**	*we do/make*
ihr	mach**t**	*you do/make*
Sie/sie	mach**en**	*you/they do/make*

1 Write in the correct form of the verb indicated. These verbs are all regular in the present tense.

(a) wir .... (*go*)

(b) er .... (*find*)

(c) sie (*singular*) .... (*sing*)

(d) ich .... (*play*)

(e) ihr .... (*do*)

(f) du .... (*say*)

(g) es .... (*come*)

(h) sie (*plural*) .... (*swim*)

(i) ich .... (*hear*)

(j) wir .... (*drink*)

Some verbs have a vowel change in the *du* and *er/sie/es/man* forms of the present tense.

2 Insert the correct form of the present tense, then translate the sentences into English.

schläfst / fahrt / esst / isst / gibt / spricht / sprecht / nimmst / liest / lest / fährt / hilfst

(a) Was .... du? (lesen)

(b) .... du? (schlafen)

(c) Annabelle .... nicht gern Fleisch. (essen)

(d) Kerstin .... gut Englisch. (sprechen)

(e) .... du Zucker? (nehmen)

(f) Ben .... bald nach Berlin. (fahren)

(g) .... du mir, bitte? (helfen)

(h) Mein Onkel .... mir 20 Euro. (geben)

....

....

....

....

....

....

....

....

3 Circle any irregular present tense verbs in this list.

er spricht / du siehst / sie macht / es liegt / ich sage / sie fährt / du kommst / er liest

Separable and reflexive verbs

> Separable verbs have two parts: a prefix and the main verb. In a sentence, the prefix goes to the end.
>
> einsteigen (*to get in*): Ich **steige** (*verb*) in das Taxi **ein** (*prefix*).

1 Fill in the two gaps in these sentences.

    (a) Wir .... bald .... (ankommen)

    (b) Er .... um 7 Uhr .... (abfahren)

    (c) Wir .... oft Filme .... (herunterladen)

    (d) Wie oft .... du .... ? (fernsehen)

    (e) Wo .... man .... ? (aussteigen)

    (f) Ich .... die Tür .... (zumachen)

> Separable verbs form the past participle as one word with the *ge-* in the middle: *ausgestiegen*.

2 Put the above sentences into the perfect tense.

    (a) ....

    (b) ....

    (c) ....

    (d) ....

    (e) ....

    (f) ....

> Reflexive verbs are always used with a reflexive pronoun (*mich*, *dich*, *sich*, etc.).
>
> ich freue **mich**   wir freuen **uns**
> du freust **dich**   ihr freut **euch**
> er/sie/es/man freut **sich**   Sie/sie freuen **sich**
>
>   Ich amüsiere **mich** gut am Computer.

3 Fill in the correct reflexive pronoun, then translate the sentences into English.

    (a) Ich interessiere .... für Geschichte.

    ....

    (b) Sara freut .... auf die Ferien.

    ....

    (c) Erinnerst du .... an mich?

    ....

    (d) Wir langweilen .... in der Schule.

    ....

    (e) Ich habe .... noch nicht entschieden.

    ....

    (f) Tina hat .... heute nicht geschminkt.

    ....

    (g) Habt ihr .... gut amüsiert?

    ....

    (h) Unser Haus befindet .... in der Nähe vom Bahnhof.

    ....

Commands

> When telling someone what to do using the *Sie* (polite) form, swap the present tense round so the verb comes before the pronoun.
>
>   Stehen Sie auf!

1 Tell someone…

    (a) …not to park here. (parken)

    ....

    (b) …not to talk so loudly. (sprechen)

    ....

    (c) …to get off here. (aussteigen)

    ....

    (d) …not to drive so fast. (fahren)

    ....

    (e) …to come in. (hereinkommen)

    ....

    (f) …to go straight on. (gehen)

    ....

    (g) …to come back soon. (kommen)

    ....

    (h) …to give you 10 euros. (geben)

    ....

> When telling someone what to do using the *du* (familiar) form, use the present tense *du* form minus the *–st* ending.
>
>   Steh auf!

2 Tell a friend…

    (a) …to get up. (aufstehen)

    ....

    (b) …to write soon. (schreiben)

    ....

    (c) …to come here. (herkommen)

    ....

    (d) …to take two. (nehmen)

    ....

    (e) …to bring you the ball. (bringen)

    ....

    (f) …to stop. (aufhören)

    ....

    (g) …to behave. (sich benehmen)

    ....

    (h) …to sit down. (sich setzen)

    ....

Present tense modals

Modal verbs (*können, müssen, wollen, dürfen, sollen, mögen*) can't be used on their own. They need to be used with the infinitive of another verb at the end of the sentence.

1 Write in the modal verb and the infinitive. Use words from the box below.

(a) Ich .... nicht schnell .... (*can't run*)

(b) Wir .... bald Kaffee .... (*must buy*)

(c) Kinder .... keinen Alkohol .... (*shouldn't drink*)

(d) Claudia .... nicht .... (*doesn't like to swim*)

(e) Schüler .... hier nicht .... (*aren't allowed to sit*)

(f) Wir .... Pommes .... (*want to eat*)

(g) Hier .... man .... (*is allowed to park*)

(h) Meine Eltern .... eine neue Wohnung ....
(*want to rent*)

(i) Du .... gut Fußball .... (*can play*)

(j) Sie (*polite*) .... höflich .... (*should be*)

darf / dürfen / kann / kannst / müssen / sollten / sollten / mag / wollen / wollen
essen / mieten / kaufen / laufen / parken / sein / sitzen / spielen / trinken / schwimmen

2 Make these sentences into modal sentences, using the verbs provided.

Man trinkt nicht zu viel. ⟶ Man **soll** nicht zu viel **trinken**.

(a) Im Kino raucht man nicht. (dürfen)

....

(b) Wir gehen zur Bowlingbahn. (mögen)

....

(c) Meine Freunde bleiben zu Hause. (wollen)

....

(d) Ihr esst weniger. (müssen)

....

(e) Man isst nicht viel Zucker. (sollen)

....

(f) Ergül spielt gut Gitarre. (können)

....

(g) Hilfst du mir bei meinen Hausaufgaben? (können)

....

(h) Man spielt hier nie. (dürfen)

....

(i) Wir fahren mit der Straßenbahn. (müssen)

....

(j) Ich esse meinen Salat nicht. (wollen)

....

Imperfect modals

> To use modals in the past, take the imperfect of the modal verb. The infinitive is sent to the end of the sentence.
>
> | müssen | musste | *had to* |
> | wollen | wollte | *wanted to* |
> | dürfen | durfte | *was allowed to* |
> | sollen | sollte | *was supposed to* |
> | mögen | mochte | *liked* |
> | können | konnte | *was able to/could* |

1 Put these present modals into the imperfect.

(a) ich will ....

(b) wir müssen ....

(c) sie können ....

(d) sie darf ....

(e) man soll ....

(f) er mag ....

(g) wir wollen ....

(h) Jutta kann ....

2 Put these modal sentences into the imperfect.

Er kann gut singen. ⟶ Er **konnte** gut singen.

(a) Du sollst gesund essen.

....

(b) Wir müssen nach Hause gehen.

....

(c) Ella mag nicht Musik hören.

....

(d) Wir wollen im Internet surfen.

....

(e) Ich kann gut Tischtennis spielen.

....

(f) Ihr dürft spät ins Bett gehen.

....

> *Möchte* (would like to) and *könnte* (could) are very useful forms. They also send the infinitive to the end.

3 Translate these sentences.

Would you like to come along? ⟶ Möchtest du mitkommen?

(a) Would you (*Sie*) like to play tennis?

....

(b) We could go shopping.

....

(c) I'd like to eat an ice cream.

....

(d) Could you (*du*) help me?

....

The perfect tense 1

> Use the perfect tense to talk about something you have done in the past.
>
> Form the perfect tense by using the verb *haben* plus the past participle at the end of the sentence.
>
>   Wir **haben** zu viel **gegessen**.

1 Unjumble these perfect tense sentences.

 (a) Wir gespielt haben Minigolf.

 ....

 (b) gekauft ihr neue Habt Schuhe?

 ....

 (c) besucht du deine Hast Oma?

 ....

 (d) Was gesagt hat er?

 ....

 (e) habe Ich gelernt Spanisch.

 ....

 (f) Hast gelesen du diese Zeitung?

 ....

 (g) ein Geschenk Dennis gegeben hat mir.

 ....

 (h) gesehen einen haben tollen Wir Film.

 ....

> Some verbs of movement use *sein* instead of *haben* to form the perfect tense.

2 Insert the correct form of *sein* and a past participle.

 (a) Wohin .... du .... ? (fahren)

 (b) Wir .... nach Mallorca .... (fahren).

 (c) Ich .... zu Hause .... (bleiben)

 (d) Usain Bolt .... schnell .... (laufen)

 (e) Meine Mutter .... nach Amerika .... (fliegen)

 (f) Der Zug .... (abfahren)

3 Circle the correct verb: *haben* or *sein*.

 (a) Abdul hat / ist 12 Stunden geschlafen.

 (b) Wir haben / sind unsere Hausaufgaben gemacht.

 (c) Wohin hast / bist du gefahren?

 (d) Ich habe / bin spät nach Hause gekommen.

 (e) Habt / Seid ihr Britta gesehen?

The perfect tense 2

Many past participles are irregular and just have to be learned.

1 What are the past participles of these common verbs?

(a) schwimmen ....

(b) sein ....

(c) schließen ....

(d) essen ....

(e) stehen ....

(f) sitzen ....

(g) schreiben ....

(h) sterben ....

(i) sprechen ....

(j) treffen ....

(k) werden ....

(l) trinken ....

(m) nehmen ....

(n) singen ....

(o) haben ....

2 Now put these sentences into the perfect tense.

Wir sehen einen Film. ⟶ Wir **haben** einen Film **gesehen**.

(a) Wir schreiben eine E-Mail.

....

(b) Wir treffen uns um 6 Uhr.

....

(c) Niemand stirbt.

....

(d) Nimmst du mein Handy?

....

(e) Ich esse eine Bratwurst.

....

(f) Er trinkt ein Glas Cola.

....

(g) Wir schwimmen im Meer.

....

(h) Marita spricht Italienisch.

....

- Separable verbs add the *ge* between the prefix and the verb.

  einladen ⟶ ein**ge**laden

- Verbs starting *be-*, *emp-*, *er-* or *ver-* don't add *ge* to the past participle.

  verstehen ⟶ verstanden

---

3 Work out the past participles of these verbs.

(a) vergessen ....

(b) ankommen ....

(c) empfehlen ....

(d) verlieren ....

(e) besuchen ....

(f) herunterladen ....

(g) abfahren ....

(h) aussteigen ....

The imperfect tense

To form the imperfect (simple past) of regular verbs, take the *–en* off the infinitive, then add *t* and the ending.

ich hör**te**	*I heard/was hearing*
du hör**test**	*you heard/were hearing*
er/sie/es/man hör**te**	*he/she/it/one heard/was hearing*
wir hör**ten**	*we heard/were hearing*
ihr hör**tet**	*you heard/were hearing*
Sie/sie hör**ten**	*you/they heard/were hearing*

1 Put these sentences into the imperfect.

Wir hören Musik. ⟶ Wir **hörten** Musik.

(a) Ich spiele am Computer.

....

(b) Was sagst du?

....

(c) Nina kauft Chips.

....

(d) Die Schüler lernen Englisch.

....

(e) Es schneit im Winter.

....

(f) Peter lacht laut.

....

Haben and *sein* have an irregular imperfect form: *hatte* and *war*, plus the appropriate endings.

2 Fill the gaps with the imperfect tense of *sein* or *haben*.

(a) Es .... gestern kalt.

(b) Wir .... auf der Party viel Spaß.

(c) Paul .... im Krankenhaus.

(d) Meine Eltern .... drei Kinder.

(e) Ich .... gestern im Imbiss.

(f) .... du Angst?

There are some irregular imperfect tense verbs which have to be learned.

3 Write **P** if the verb is in the present tense and **I** if it is in the imperfect.

(a) Es gab viel zu essen.   ....   (g) Sie kamen um 6 Uhr an.   ....

(b) Wir sitzen im Kino.   ....   (h) Wie findest du das?   ....

(c) Es tut mir leid!   ....   (i) Aua! Das tat weh!   ....

(d) Ich fahre nach Berlin.   ....   (j) Ich fand es gut.   ....

(e) Er kommt früh an.   ....   (k) Es gibt nicht viel zu tun.   ....

(f) Er saß im Wohnzimmer.   ....   (l) Klaus fuhr zu schnell.   ....

The future tense

It is quite normal to use the present tense to indicate the future.

Ich komme bald nach Hause. *I'm coming home soon.*

1 Use the present tense to indicate the future. Put the future expression straight after the verb.

Wir (gehen) einkaufen (morgen). ⟶ Wir gehen morgen einkaufen.

(a) Susi (gehen) auf die Uni (nächstes Jahr).

....

(b) Wir (fahren) nach Ibiza (im Sommer).

....

(c) Er (kommen) zu uns (übermorgen).

....

(d) Ich (bleiben) zu Hause (heute Abend).

....

(e) (Bringen) du deine Schwester mit (am Wochenende)?

....

To form the actual future tense, use the present tense of *werden* with the infinitive at the end of the sentence.

ich werde	wir werden
du wirst	ihr werdet
er/sie/es/man wird	Sie/sie werden

2 Insert the correct form of *werden* and the appropriate infinitive from the box below.

Olaf **wird** Cola **trinken**.

(a) Ich .... um 6 Uhr .... (*leave*)

(b) .... du am Wochenende Musik ....? (*listen*)

(c) .... ihr Pizza ....? (*eat*)

(d) Wir .... die Prüfung .... (*pass*)

(e) Nächstes Jahr .... wir nach Afrika .... (*travel*)

(f) Daniel .... einen Film .... (*download*)

(g) Ich .... ein Problem mit meinem Laptop .... (*have*)

(h) Bayern München .... das Spiel .... (*win*)

(i) Meine Freunde .... um 9 Uhr .... (*arrive*)

(j) Meine Schwester .... im August .... (*get married*)

heiraten / reisen / hören / essen / herunterladen / gewinnen / haben / ankommen / abfahren / bestehen

3 Write three sentences about things you will do in the future.

(a) ....

....

(b) ....

....

(c) ....

....

The conditional

> To form the conditional, use part of *würde* plus the infinitive at the end.
>
> | ich würde | wir würden |
> |---|---|
> | du würdest | ihr würdet |
> | er/sie/es/man würde | Sie/sie würden |

1　Fill in the correct part of *würde*.

(a)　Wenn wir Zeit hätten, ... wir einkaufen gehen.

(b)　Wenn meine Eltern Geld hätten, ... sie ein Auto kaufen.

(c)　Wenn ich Kinder hätte, ... ich sie lieben.

(d)　Wenn Tanja nicht krank wäre, ... sie Skateboard fahren.

(e)　Wenn du fleißiger wärst, ... du deine Prüfung bestehen.

(f)　Wenn das Wetter besser wäre, ... wir Sport treiben.

> The conditional of *haben* is *hätte*, with the appropriate endings. The conditional of *sein* is *wäre*, with the appropriate endings.

2　Put in the right form of *hätte* or *wäre*.

(a)　Wenn ich Krankenschwester ...., würde ich mich freuen.

(b)　Wenn er Klempner ...., würde er viel verdienen.

(c)　Wenn wir in einer Fabrik arbeiten würden, ... wir müde.

(d)　Wenn wir Glasflaschen ...., würden wir sie recyceln.

(e)　Wenn ich Hunger ...., würde ich eine Bratwurst essen.

(f)　Wenn Manya und Timo Talent ...., würden sie in einer Band spielen.

> | ich möchte | *I would like* |
> |---|---|
> | ich hätte gern | *I would like to have* |

3　Write three sentences about things you'd like to do. Start with *Ich möchte...*

(a)　..

　　..

(b)　..

　　..

(c)　..

　　..

4　Write three sentences about things you'd like to have. Start with *Ich hätte gern...*

(a)　..

　　..

(b)　..

　　..

(c)　..

　　..

The pluperfect tense

> To form the pluperfect, (i.e. what *had* happened), use the imperfect form of *haben* or *sein* plus the past participle at the end.
>
> ich hatte (*I had,* etc.)   wir hatten
> du hattest   ihr hattet
> er/sie/man hatte   Sie/sie hatten
>
>   Ich **hatte** mein Buch vergessen.   *I had forgotten my book.*

1   Put in the right part of *haben* or *sein*, plus a past participle, to make these sentences pluperfect.

(a)   Wir .... Kaffee und Kuchen .... (*had ordered*)

(b)   .... du Spaß .... ? (*had had*)

(c)   Ich .... eine neue Stelle .... (*had got*)

(d)   Wir .... unsere Freunde .... (*had invited*)

(e)   Als ich nach Hause .... (*had come*), habe ich gegessen.

(f)   Kagan .... zur Bäckerei .... (*had gone*)

(g)   Sie (*plural*) .... zu Hause .... (*had stayed*)

(h)   Ich .... mit dem Auto nach Frankfurt .... (*had driven*)

2   Write out these perfect tense sentences in the pluperfect. You only need to change the part of *haben* or *sein*.

(a)   Es ist nicht passiert.

     ....

(b)   Ich habe dir eine E-Mail geschickt.

     ....

(c)   Hast du dich nicht geschminkt?

     ....

(d)   Ich bin sehr früh eingeschlafen.

     ....

(e)   Opa ist noch nie nach London gefahren.

     ....

(f)   Bist du zur Haltestelle gegangen?

     ....

(g)   Wir haben unseren Müll zur Mülldeponie gebracht.

     ....

(h)   Er hat zwei Computerspiele heruntergeladen.

     ....

(i)   Die Fabrik ist sehr laut gewesen.

     ....

(j)   Fatima hat Abitur gemacht.

     ....

Questions

> To ask a simple question, just swap the pronoun (or name) and the verb around.
>
>   Du bist krank. ⟶ Bist du krank?

1 Make these statements into questions.

  (a) Kevin spielt oft am Computer.

....

  (b) Du hast dein Handy verloren.

....

  (c) Wir wollen Volleyball spielen.

....

  (d) Hakan studiert Informatik.

....

  (e) Ihr geht morgen zum Sportzentrum.

....

2 Ask the questions to which these are the answers.

   Ja, ich habe Chips gekauft. ⟶ Hast du Chips gekauft?

  (a) Nein, ich bin nicht zum Supermarkt gefahren.

....

  (b) Ja, Ayse wird Chemie studieren.

....

  (c) Nein, mein Auto ist nicht kaputt.

....

  (d) Ja, ich esse gern Bratwurst mit Pommes.

....

  (e) Ich weiß nicht, ob es morgen regnen wird.

....

> You have to learn the German question words.

3 Draw lines to link the English and German question words.

who?	wessen?
what?	wie viele?
how?	warum?
when?	was für?
why?	wer?
where?	mit wem?
how many?	wie?
what kind of?	wann?
whose?	was?
who with?	wo?

4 Write three questions you could ask during a role play about visiting a town.

  (a) ....

  (b) ....

  (c) ....

Time markers

> Time markers are useful words for showing when something happens, did happen or will happen.

1 Write what tense (present, past or future) these time markers indicate.

(a) gestern   ....   (f) normalerweise   ....

(b) früher   ....   (g) vor zwei Wochen ....

(c) bald   ....   (h) morgen   ....

(d) letzte Woche ....   (i) nächste Woche   ....

(e) heute   ....   (j) jetzt   ....

2 Draw lines to link the English and German expressions.

1 manchmal   A *immediately*
2 neulich   B *on time*
3 sofort   C *sometimes*
4 täglich   D *in the future*
5 rechtzeitig   E *recently*
6 in Zukunft   F *every day*

3 Rewrite these sentences using the time expressions provided. Put the time expression first and the verb second.

Wir fahren nach Bremen. (morgen) ⟶ Morgen fahren wir nach Bremen.

(a) Ich werde mein Betriebspraktikum machen. (nächste Woche)

....

....

(b) Ulli sieht fern. (heute Abend)

....

....

(c) Man wird Strom sparen. (in Zukunft)

....

....

(d) Du wirst einen Unfall haben. (bald)

....

....

(e) Wir treffen uns mit unseren Freunden. (manchmal)

....

....

(f) Ich war bei meinem Onkel. (neulich)

....

....

(g) Metin hat sein Betriebspraktikum begonnen. (vorgestern)

....

....

(h) Ich gehe zur Bäckerei. (jeden Tag)

....

....

Numbers

> Revise the numbers 1–1000. You need to be completely confident in using numbers.

1 Write the German numbers in figures.

(a) vierhunderteinundzwanzig   ....

(b) tausendsechshundertvierundvierzig   ....

(c) achtundsechzig   ....

(d) dreihunderteins   ....

(e) siebenundneunzig   ....

(f) hundertfünf   ....

(g) siebzehn   ....

(h) sechshundertdreiundfünfzig   ....

2 Choose the correct cardinal number to fill each gap by drawing a linking line.

1 Es ist .... nach .... (20, 9)   A   sieben

2 Ausverkauf! .... Prozent Rabatt! (15)   B   zwölf

3 Es ist .... Grad. (13)   C   dreißig

4 Ich habe .... Euro gewonnen. (650)   D   fünfzehn

5 Der Zug kommt um .... Minuten vor .... an. (12, 7)   E   dreizehn

6 Es gibt .... Schüler in meiner Klasse. (30)   F   sechshundertfünfzig

   G   neun

   H   zwanzig

> Revise the ordinal numbers.

1st	erste	20th	zwanzigste
2nd	zweite	21st	einundzwanzigste
3rd	dritte	30th	dreißigste
4th	vierte	31st	einunddreißigste
5th	fünfte		
6th	sechste		
7th	siebte		

3 Write the dates in numbers.

der einunddreißigste Mai ⟶ 31.5.

(a) der zwölfte März   ....

(b) der dreizehnte Juli   ....

(c) der achtundzwanzigste Dezember   ....

(d) der erste April   ....

(e) der dritte Januar   ....

(f) der siebzehnte Juni   ....

4 Write in the ordinal numbers.

(a) Mein Geburtstag ist am .... November. (*1st*)

(b) Saschas Geburtstag ist am .... September. (*7th*)

(c) Das Konzert findet am .... Mai statt. (*12th*)

(d) Die Ferien beginnen am .... Juli. (*2nd*)

Test: Listening 1

Pearson Edexcel publishes official Sample Assessment Material on its website. This test has been written to help you practise what you have learned across the four skills, and may not be representative of a real exam paper.

Shopping for clothes

LISTENING TRACK 58

Listen to the recording

1 Petra is talking about her shopping trip.

What does she say?

Listen to the recording and complete the sentences by putting a cross [×] in the correct box for each question.

(i) Petra tries on a clothes item which is …

☐	**A** reduced
☐	**B** striped
☐	**C** yellow
☐	**D** dark

(1 mark)

(ii) Petra is looking for size …

☐	**A** 38
☐	**B** 28
☐	**C** 36
☐	**D** 34

(1 mark)

(iii) Petra is going to try …

☐	**A** a catalogue
☐	**B** another day
☐	**C** online
☐	**D** the department store

(1 mark)

Work experience

LISTENING TRACK 59

Listen to the recording

2 Your German exchange partner is talking about what his friends are doing on their work experience placements.

What does he say about them?

Listen to the recording and put a cross [×] in each one of the **three** correct boxes.

A	has to get up early	☐
B	can have a lie-in	☐
C	eats at the workplace	☐
D	goes home for lunch	☐
E	is enjoying work experience	☐
F	finds work experience boring	☐
G	is working in a shop	☐

(3 marks)

Test: Listening 2

Friends

1 You hear a discussion about members of a clique.

What three things are said about Oli?

Listen to the recording and put a cross [x] in each one of the **three** correct boxes.

Listen to the recording

A	Oli cheats.	☐
B	Oli is patient.	☐
C	Oli gets into trouble.	☐
D	Oli is a good listener.	☐
E	Oli is often busy.	☐
F	Oli breaks the rules.	☐
G	The group is important to Oli.	☐

(3 marks)

Urlaub

2 Du hörst dieses Interview mit der Managerin eines Reisebüros.

Füll die Lücke in jedem Satz mit einem Wort aus dem Kasten. Es gibt mehr Wörter als Lücken.

Listen to the recording

> zuverlässig   Viertel   Hotel   gleichen   unterschiedlich
> Österreich   überrascht   Drittel   langweilt   Ausland

(a) Manche Leute fahren gern ins .... **(1 mark)**

(b) Spanien ist auf dem .... Platz wie im vorigen Jahr. **(1 mark)**

(c) Das Klima in Spanien ist .... gut. **(1 mark)**

(d) Ein .... der Kunden hat einen Urlaub in Amerika gebucht. **(1 mark)**

(e) Der amerikanische Lebensstil .... deutsche Besucher. **(1 mark)**

Test: Listening 3

At school

1 You hear an interview on the school radio with Melina talking about her classmates.

Listen to the interview and answer the following questions **in English.** You do not need to write in full sentences.

(a) Give **one** example of how Ivan showed he was shy last year.

.... **(1 mark)**

(b) How has Melina's attitude to Ivan changed?

.... **(1 mark)**

(c) What was Olivia's behaviour like in class last year? Give **two** examples.

....

.... **(2 marks)**

(d) What reason is given for Olivia becoming friendlier?

.... **(1 mark)**

Advantages of sport

2 You hear a report about sport and young people on Swiss radio.

What does the report say about sport?

Listen to the recording and put a cross [×] in each one of the **three** correct boxes.

A	Physical activity is popular with young people.	☐
B	A sedentary lifestyle is more popular than an active one.	☐
C	Scientists research inactive lifestyles.	☐
D	Team and individual sports have the same effect.	☐
E	Sport makes some people cross.	☐
F	People should turn off their computers at bedtime.	☐
G	Sport reduces stress levels.	☐

(3 marks)

Listen to the recording

Listen to the recording

Test: Speaking 1

1 Complete the Speaking task, using the recorded prompts to help you.

> **Topic: Transport and travel**
>
> **Instructions to candidates:**
>
> You are booking a train ticket at the station to go and visit a friend.
>
> The teacher will play the role of the ticket office employee and will speak first.
>
> You must address the employee as *Sie*.
>
> You will talk to the teacher using the five prompts below.
>
> - where you see – **?** – you must ask a question
> - where you see – **!** – you must respond to something you have not prepared
>
> **Task**
>
> **Sie sind am Hamburger Hauptbahnhof und wollen eine Zugkarte kaufen. Sie sprechen mit dem Beamten / der Beamtin.**
>
> 1. Fahrt – wann und wohin
> 2. Fahrt – Grund
> 3. **!**
> 4. Fahrkarte – was
> 5. **?** Preis

Listen to the recording

Once you have prepared and practised your answer, listen to the sample role play in the Answers section for more ideas on what you could include.

2 Complete the Speaking task, using the recorded prompts to help you.

> **Topic: Technology**
>
> **Instructions to candidates:**
>
> You are talking with your exchange partner about computer usage at home. The teacher will play the role of your exchange partner and will speak first.
>
> You must address your exchange partner as *du*.
>
> You will talk to the teacher using the five prompts below.
>
> - where you see – **?** – you must ask a question
> - where you see – **!** – you must respond to something you have not prepared
>
> **Task**
>
> **Du sprichst mit deinem Austauschpartner/deiner Austauschpartnerin über Computer.**
>
> 1. Online-Aktivitäten – zwei
> 2. Computerspiele – Meinung, Grund
> 3. **!**
> 4. **?** Computer – wie oft
> 5. **?** Online-Pläne – heute Abend

Listen to the recording

Once you have prepared and practised your answer, listen to the sample role play in the answers section for more ideas on what you could include.

Test: Speaking 2

Topic: The environment

1 Complete the picture-based task.

Schau dir das Foto an und sei bereit, über Folgendes zu sprechen:

- Beschreibung des Fotos
- Deine Meinung zum Umweltschutz
- Wie umweltfreundlich du letzte Woche warst
- Wie du in Zukunft umweltfreundlicher sein wirst
- Das größte Problem für den Planeten

> When you have prepared your answer, listen to the sample dialogue in the answer section for ideas on what you could include.

2 Schau dir das Foto an und sei bereit, über Folgendes zu sprechen:

- Beschreibung des Fotos
- Ob dir Umweltschutz wichtig ist
- Wie umweltfreundlich du letzte Woche warst
- Wie du umweltfreundlicher werden könntest
- !

> Choose whether you want to do the Foundation version (question 1) or Higher version (question 2). Or, for extra practice, do both!

Test: Reading 1

School

1   Read these profiles on the class 10 website.

Lena	Ich bin sehr lustig und sehr freundlich. Ich bin nie schlecht gelaunt und ich habe viele Freunde in der Klasse.
Yusuf	Ich bin sehr intelligent, aber ich kann in der Klasse schüchtern sein. Ich spreche nicht gern mit den Lehrern und ich bin oft ängstlich.
Halina	Ich bin fleißig und mache immer meine Hausaufgaben. In der Pause gehe ich oft in die Bibliothek. Ich lese dort gern.
Frank	Ich bin musikalisch und lade gern Lieder aus dem Internet herunter. Ich spiele Gitarre und singe die ganze Zeit.

Who says what about themselves? Enter either **Lena, Yusuf, Halina** or **Frank**.

You can use each person more than once.

(a) .... likes books.   **(1 mark)**

(b) .... listens to songs.   **(1 mark)**

(c) .... is sociable.   **(1 mark)**

(d) .... lacks confidence.   **(1 mark)**

(e) .... is diligent.   **(1 mark)**

(f) .... has difficulty with adults.   **(1 mark)**

Environment

2   Translate this passage **into English**.

Meine Mutter spart immer Energie. Zu Hause tragen wir alle warme Pullis. Das ist nervig, weil ich lieber T-Shirts trage. Letzten Mittwoch habe ich den Müll nicht getrennt. Nächste Woche werde ich das jeden Tag machen.

....

....

....

....

....

....

....   **(7 marks)**

Test: Reading 2

Sport

1 Read this article from a German website.

> ● ● ●
>
> Teenager heute genießen eine breite Auswahl an Sportarten in der Schule. Das gab es früher nicht.
>
> Viele Jugendliche legen großen Wert darauf, ein gesundes Leben zu führen, und deshalb ist es ihnen wichtig, regelmäßig zu trainieren und Sport zu treiben.
>
> Mehr als 45% aller Jugendlichen gehören entweder einer Sport-AG oder einem Sportverein an. Früher haben solche Gelegenheiten für junge Leute nicht existiert. Man musste warten, bis man älter war.
>
> Hoffentlich geht dieser Trend im Sportbereich so weiter! Dann werden wir wirklich ein aktives Land haben!

Answer the following questions in **English**. You do not need to write in full sentences.

(a) Why do young people regard sport as important? .... **(1 mark)**

(b) How are they unlike their parents as regards sport? .... **(1 mark)**

(c) Why will it be good if this fashion continues? .... **(1 mark)**

Part-time work

2 Read this article from a German newspaper.

> Thomas studiert Fremdsprachen an der Uni. Früher hat er am Wochenende und in den Ferien in einem Freizeitzentrum gearbeitet, was ihm besonders gut gefallen hat. Leider hat das Zentrum einen neuen Chef, der keine Studenten im Team haben will.
>
> Thomas musste sich einen anderen Job suchen, um Geld zu verdienen, und er hat sich in mehreren Geschäften in der Stadt beworben. Aber alles ohne Erfolg.
>
> In den Sommerferien wird Thomas jetzt als Küchenhilfe in einem Schnellimbiss in der Stadtmitte arbeiten. Er war sehr froh, als er den Job bekommen hat, aber das Gehalt ist sehr niedrig.

Put a cross [×] in the correct box.

(i) Thomas found the job at the sports centre …

☐	**A** different
☐	**B** difficult
☐	**C** tiring
☐	**D** good

(1 mark)

(ii) Thomas lost the job due to …

☐	**A** the centre closing
☐	**B** an argument
☐	**C** new management
☐	**D** negligence

(1 mark)

(iii) Thomas … a retail job.

☐	**A** did not want
☐	**B** could not find
☐	**C** disliked the thought of
☐	**D** was successful with

(1 mark)

(iv) Thomas will work in a …

☐	**A** food outlet
☐	**B** factory
☐	**C** sports centre
☐	**D** office

(1 mark)

(v) Thomas was disappointed by the …

☐	**A** uniform
☐	**B** location
☐	**C** wages
☐	**D** working hours

(1 mark)

Test: Reading 3

Die unendliche Geschichte by Michael Ende

1   Read the extract from the text.

While fleeing from his schoolmates, Bastian seeks refuge in a shop.

»Ich heiße Bastian«, sagte der Junge, »Bastian Balthasar Bux.«

»Ziemlich kurioser Name«, knurrte der Mann, »mit diesen drei B's. Ich heiße Karl Konrad Koreander.«

»Das sind drei K's«, sagte der Junge ernst.

»Hm«, brummte der Alte, »stimmt!«

»Jetzt möchte ich nur noch eins wissen, nämlich wieso du vorhin mit solchem Krach in meinen Laden eingebrochen bist. ... Ich hatte den Eindruck, dass du auf der Flucht wärst.«

Bastian nickte. Sein rundes Gesicht wurde plötzlich noch blasser und seine Augen noch etwas größer.

»Wahrscheinlich hast du eine Ladenkasse ausgeraubt. ... Ist die Polizei hinter dir her, mein Kind?«

Answer the following questions in **English**. You do not need to write in full sentences.

(a) What does Bastian have in common with the old man?

.... **(1 mark)**

(b) How did Bastian enter the shop?

.... **(1 mark)**

(c) What impression did Bastian's entrance make on the old man?

.... **(1 mark)**

(d) What indication does Bastian give that he is afraid?

.... **(1 mark)**

(e) What crime does the old man think Bastian has committed?

.... **(1 mark)**

Had a go ☐   **Nearly there** ☐   **Nailed it!** ☐

Test: Reading 4

Familie

1   Lies Alis Blog über seine Familie.

● ● ●	
Vater	Seitdem mein Vater meine Stiefmutter geheiratet hat, gibt es immer Krach zwischen uns. Sie ist eifersüchtig und mag es nicht, wenn mein Vater mit mir alleine Zeit verbringt.
Stiefmutter	Ich kenne meine Stiefmutter erst seit vier Jahren und wir verstehen uns gar nicht gut. Letzten Samstag hat sie verlangt, dass ich meinen Halbbruder babysitten sollte.
Schwester	Vor drei Jahren ist meine Schwester in ihre eigene Wohnung in die Stadtmitte gezogen, weil sie es zu Hause nicht länger aushalten konnte. Ich vermisse sie sehr.
Halbbruder	Mein kleiner Halbbruder hat lockige blonde Haare. Er sieht zwar sehr süß aus, aber er ist total nervig.

Wer ist das? Trag entweder **Vater**, **Stiefmutter**, **Schwester** oder **Halbbruder** ein.
Du kannst jedes Wort mehr als einmal verwenden.

(a)   Alis .... benimmt sich anders als er aussieht.   **(1 mark)**

(b)   Alis .... lebt jetzt selbstständig.   **(1 mark)**

(c)   Alis .... benimmt sich seit der Hochzeit anders.   **(1 mark)**

(d)   Alis .... hat sich mit Ali nie gut verstanden.   **(1 mark)**

(e)   Alis .... fehlt ihm.   **(1 mark)**

Translation

2   Translate this passage **into English**.

Mein Vater ist Arzt auf dem Land. Er muss oft nachts arbeiten und kommt dann erschöpft nach Hause. Er würde viel lieber eine andere Stelle haben, wo die Arbeitsstunden kürzer sind. Er hatte früher einen Teilzeitjob in einem Laden in der Stadtmitte, was ihm sehr gut gefallen hat.

....

....

....

....

....

....

....

....

....

....

....   **(7 marks)**

Test: Writing 1

Am Campingplatz

1 Du bist auf dem Campingplatz. Du postest dieses Foto online für deine Freunde.

Beschreib das Foto **und** schreib deine Meinung über Urlaub auf dem Campingplatz.

Schreib ungefähr 20–30 Wörter **auf Deutsch.**

....

....

....

....   **(12 marks)**

An der Schule

2 Schreib eine E-Mail an deine Brieffreundin und beschreib deine Sekundarschule.

Schreib:
- wo die Schule ist
- wie das Gebäude ist
- was man in der Pause machen kann
- Events an der Schule im nächsten Halbjahr.

Schreib ungefähr 40–50 Wörter **auf Deutsch.**

Hallo Sura, ...

....

....

....

....

....

....   **(16 marks)**

Das Essen

3 Übersetze **ins Deutsche**.

   (a) I like eating chips.

   .... **(2 marks)**

   (b) My brother never eats meat.

   .... **(2 marks)**

   (c) My favourite dessert is cake with chocolate sauce.

   .... **(2 marks)**

   (d) At the weekend I drank a big bottle of cola.

   .... **(3 marks)**

   (e) In the evening I was ill and we went to the hospital.

   .... **(3 marks)**

Ostern

4 Übersetze **ins Deutsche**.

> Last Easter my parents hid lots of eggs in the garden. Every time I found an egg, my brother took it straight away. Next year I won't look for any chocolate, because it is very unhealthy. I would rather spend the money on clothes, which are much more useful.

   ....

   ....

   ....

   ....

   ....

   ....

   .... **(12 marks)**

Test: Writing 2

Mein Zuhause

1 Dein Freund Sadi schickt dir Fragen über dein Zuhause.

Schreib eine Antwort an Sadi.

> Write your answers for this section on a separate piece of paper if you need more space.

Du **musst** über diese Punkte schreiben:

- seit wann du hier wohnst
- Aktivität letztes Wochenende zu Hause
- deine Pläne für Sommerferien zu Hause
- warum Sadi dich besuchen soll.

Schreib ungefähr 80–90 Wörter **auf Deutsch**.

....

....

....

....

....

....

....

....

....

....

....

....

....

....

....

....

....

....

....

....

.... **(20 marks)**

Had a go ☐   Nearly there ☐   Nailed it! ☐

Geld sammeln

2 Du nimmst an einem gesponserten Marathonlauf für ein Wasserprojekt in Afrika teil.

Du machst ein Poster für die Schule, damit alle Schüler dir Geld dafür spenden.

Du **musst** über diese Punkte schreiben:

- Details über das Projekt
- warum man dafür Geld spenden sollte
- wie du schon Geld gesammelt hast
- wie die Schüler helfen könnten.

Rechtfertige deine Ideen und Meinungen.

Schreib ungefähr 130–150 Wörter **auf Deutsch.**

Ein Marathonlauf für ein Wasserprojekt in Afrika! ....

....

....

....

....

....

....

....

....

....

....

....

....

....

....

....

....

....

....

....

.... **(28 marks)**

Answers

Topic 1 Identity and culture

1. Physical descriptions
1   (a) Robert, (b) Nils, (c) Eymen, (d) Taiji, (e) Nils,
    (f) Robert
2   A, E, G

2. Character descriptions
1   B, E, G
2   (i) D, (ii) B, (iii) A

3. Family
1   (i) B, (ii) A, (iii) D, (iv) C, (v) D
2   A, D

4. Friends
1   Sample translation:
    (a) Ich liebe meine Freunde / Freundinnen.
    (b) Meine Freundin Lotti ist sehr nett / sympathisch.
    (c) Sie wohnt neben dem Bahnhof in Berlin.
    (d) Letzte Woche sind wir zusammen ins Kino
        gegangen / gefahren.
    (e) Wir haben viel gelacht, weil wir einen lustigen Film
        gesehen haben.
2   Sample translation:
    Gestern habe ich meinen Freund Yusuf besucht, um
    Computerspiele zu spielen. Sein Bruder ist sehr ärgerlich.
    Yusuf kommt oft zu mir nach Hause, aber ich will, dass er
    alleine kommt. Ich verbringe lieber Zeit mit Yusuf, weil wir uns
    sehr gut verstehen.

5. Role models
1   (a) musical   (b) many
    (c) gifts   (d) study
    (e) well
2   B, D, G

6. Relationships
1   Sample translation:
    My brother gets on my nerves. In the evenings he listens
    to music. That is bad because I prefer to practise the piano.
    Yesterday I went to a concert with my friends.
    At the weekend we are staying at home.
2   (i) B, (ii) D, (iii) B

7. When I was younger
1   1 B, 2 C, 3 A, 4 D
2   Student's own answers

8. Peer group
1   (a) gives description of photo, but no opinion
    (b) is just right
    (c) is not long enough
    (d) is too long
    (e) gives opinion but no description of photo
2   Student's own answers

9. Customs
1   (a) right, (b) polite, (c) you, (d) understand, (e) fast
2   (a) difference in educational system between Germany and China
    (b) at work
    (c) German discipline
    (d) do a language course / be prepared for meeting/seeing lots of
        Chinese people

10. Home
1   (a) was sitting in front of the desk, rather than behind it
    (b) desk facing window to provide privacy / a screen from
        the room

    (c) with his back
    (d) behind him
    (e) that Charlie had invited him

11. Everyday life
1   Part (a)   Part (b)
    (i) A, (ii) B, (iii) D   (i) D , (ii) C, (iii) A

12. Meals at home
1   (a) put on coffee machine
    (b) shortly after 8.15 / shortly after a quarter past eight
    (c) one of: flowers / fresh napkins / fresh tablecloth
    (d) one of: marmalade / toast
    (e) things were going to change for ever / never stay the same
2   A, D, G

13. Food and drink
1   (i) A, (ii) B, (iii) D, (iv) C, (v) D
2   A, D, G

14. Shopping for clothes
1   Sample translation:
    Buying clothes can be very tiring. You can buy good value
    garments / items of clothing at the department store and also at
    the market. I would suggest to all customers that they always try
    on the clothes properly in the changing room. You can change the
    purchases if there is a problem.
2   (a) Familienmitglied, (b) dunkle, (c) 31., (d) Größen, (e) 49

15. Social media
1   Part (a)
    (i)   one of: entertaining / dangerous
    (ii) 89% have a profile (It is not correct to write: one
          network / profile)
    (iii) it has been going on for a long time (It is not correct to write:
          talking with people / communicating)
    (iv) you can tell how old the person really is (It is not correct to
          write: get to know person)
    Part (b)
    (i)   parent-free
    (ii) started a new homepage
    (iii) teenagers should have private lives / privacy; they
          need to relax
    (iv) will backfire / cause bigger problems in the future

16. Technology
1   (i) D, (ii) A, (iii) A, (iv) C, (v) B

17. Online activities
1   Sample answer:
    Teacher: Beschreib mir das Foto.
    Student: Das Bild zeigt ein Mädchen,
    das auf seinem Bett liegt. Sie ist ein
    Teenager und sie hat lange glatte Haare. Sie trägt
    Kopfhörer, und sie lächelt, weil sie glücklich ist.
    Im Vordergrund hat sie einen Computer, aber sie
    benutzt ihn nicht, weil sie sich auf das Handy konzentriert.
    Das Mädchen trägt einen hellen Pullover und ihr Schlafzimmer
    sieht schön aus.
    Teacher: Ich finde Online-Aktivitäten toll. Was meinst du?
    Student: Ich finde Online-Aktivitäten super, weil sie so praktisch
    sind. Wenn ich Probleme mit den Hausaufgaben habe, suche ich
    die Informationen sofort im Internet. Es ist auch gut, dass man
    Kinokarten online kaufen kann, weil das Zeit spart.

SPEAKING TRACK 66   Listen to the recording

Schlecht daran ist aber, dass man vielleicht zu viel Zeit am Bildschirm verbringt. Es ist sicher gefährlich, wenn man stundenlang am Computer sitzt.

Teacher: Welche Online-Aktivitäten hast du gestern gemacht? Erzähl mir davon.

Student: Gestern Abend hatte ich keine Hausaufgaben, also habe ich Computerspiele online gespielt. Das hat echt viel Spaß gemacht, weil das Spiel sehr spannend war. Ich habe auch online mit Freunden gechattet und wir haben zusammen etwas für nächstes Wochenende geplant. Ich habe auch eine E-Mail an meinen Austauschpartner geschrieben, um seiner Familie für meinen Besuch bei ihm zu danken.

Teacher: Was willst du heute Abend online machen?

Student: Heute Abend muss ich leider zuerst meine Hausaufgaben am Computer machen. Wir haben zu Hause einen Desktop-PC mit Farbdrucker, und hier kann man am besten die Hausaufgaben machen, finde ich. Ich habe auch ein Smartphone, und das ist so gut wie ein Computer. Heute Abend will ich Musik herunterladen, soziale Netzwerke besuchen und mit Freunden simsen. Ich habe keine Konsole zu Hause, aber ich kann manche Spiele am Computer spielen. Oder ich kann meinen Freund besuchen und bei ihm spielen. Er hat eine tolle Konsole!

Teacher: Wie findest du Technologie?

Student: Meiner Meinung nach langweilt man sich nie, wenn man Technologie hat. Man kann sich entweder lustige Videoclips ansehen oder Lieder herunterladen. Mit Technologie kann man jederzeit in Kontakt mit Freunden aus der ganzen Welt bleiben, und das ist immer interessant. Ohne Technologie muss das Leben sehr langweilig und einsam sein. Für meine Generation ist es schwer, sich ein Leben ohne Technologie vorzustellen.

18. For and against technology
1   Sample translation:
The internet is fun, but it is also dangerous. The biggest advantage for me is that I can stay in touch with relatives everywhere in the world. But I don't do internet shopping / shop online. Last year somebody stole my personal details and that is a risk of virtual life.
2   A, C, D

19. Hobbies
1   (a) piano
    (b) garage
    (c) two of: rock / dance / classical
2   (a) toll, (b) toll, (c) langweilig, (d) gefährlich,
    (e) anstrengend

20. Interests
1   (a) Hobbys von jungen Leuten
    (b) drei Tage
    (c) um Geld zu verdienen / um einen Beruf zu finden / für die Arbeit
    (d) Freizeitaktivitäten müssen Spaß machen / ihr gefallen / Freude machen
    (e) one of: Informationen / kostenlose Dinge / Artikel

21. Music
1   Part (a)   Part (b)
    (i) C, (ii) D, (iii) A   (i) B, (ii) A, (iii) C

22 Sport
2   Sample answer:
Es gibt einen gut ausgestatteten Fitnessraum und eine Sporthalle. Besonders positiv ist das Schwimmbad, wo man Wassersport treiben kann. Jeder kann an einer großen Auswahl an Sportarten teil nehmen.
Natürlich sollt ihr nach dem Event noch weiter Sport treiben. Es wäre also toll, einmal pro Monat einen Sporttag zu organisieren, wo man wieder Sportarten ausprobieren kann. Man müsste dafür keine Eintrittskarte kaufen.

23. Reading
1   (i) C, (ii) A, (iii) B, (iv) C, (v) A
2   (a) mountains
    (b) she knows it herself
    (c) knowledge of Alps / villages and towns in Alps

24. Films
1   (a) former / retired vet
    (b) father and daughter both in it
    (c) waste of money
    (d) doesn't want to break the law
    (e) the subtitles were annoying

25. Television
1   (a) exciting, (b) thriller, (c) last, (d) cross, (e) different
2   (a) films
    (b) modern / up-to-date

26. Celebrations
1   Sample translation:
We are celebrating a wedding / marriage. Today my aunt is marrying her partner. That is wonderful, because she loves him. Yesterday I bought a new dress. It is great that the whole family is together.
2   (i) D, (ii) A, (iii) C, (iv) B, (v) D

27. Festivals
1   (i) D, (ii) A, (iii) B, (iv) C, (v) C

Topic 2 Local area, holiday and travel

28. Holiday preferences
Sample answer:
Teacher: Guten Tag. Wollen Sie in Urlaub fahren?
Student: Ja, ich interessiere mich für eine Woche Urlaub in Spanien.
Teacher: Welche Unterkunft möchten Sie haben?
Student: Ich möchte am liebsten in einem Hotel bleiben.
Teacher: Haben Sie schon einmal einen Urlaub am Meer gemacht?
Student: Ja, ich war letztes Jahr in Korsika an der Küste.
Teacher: Schön. Haben Sie eine Frage?
Student: Was kostet der Urlaub, bitte?
Teacher: 600 Euro. Haben Sie noch eine Frage?
Student: Was kann man abends in dieser Gegend machen?
Teacher: Das finden Sie in der Broschüre.

SPEAKING TRACK 67

Listen to the recording

29. Hotels
Sample answer:
Teacher: Was wollen Sie reservieren?
Student: Ich will ein Doppelzimmer reservieren, bitte.
Teacher: Wann kommen Sie an?
Student: Ich komme am Donnerstagabend an.
Teacher: Was wollen Sie zum Frühstück essen?
Student: Wurst mit Brot, bitte.
Teacher: Wie fahren Sie zu uns?
Student: Ich fahre mit dem Auto.
Teacher: Schön. Haben Sie eine Frage?
Student: Wie viel kostet das Zimmer, bitte?
Teacher: Es kostet 125 Euro pro Nacht.

SPEAKING TRACK 68

Listen to the recording

30. Campsites

1 (a) May, (b) towels, (c) nature, (d) quiet, (e) tent
2 (a) it's in the best area
  (b) have to be quiet at night / not make noise
  (c) will be in a hotel with discos at the pool at night

31. Accommodation

1 (a) Wohnblock, (b) Gasthaus, (c) Hotel, (d) Bauernhof,
  (e) Wohnblock
2 (a) youth hostel
  (b) sharing a room / dormitory
  (c) price / cheap
  (d) a family / families

32. Holiday destinations

1 (a) many interesting countries and holiday regions
  (b) any / all
  (c) the coast and small islands of Spain
2 (a) August, (b) typische, (c) Wetters, (d) Kosten, (e) Küche

33. Holiday experiences

1 Sample translation:
  In the winter holidays my family goes skiing / on a skiing
  holiday. We are on the slopes / piste the whole day.
  The view is great when the sun shines. Last time nobody had to go
  to hospital. Next year I will go on holiday with friends.
2 B, E

34. Holiday activities

1 Student's own answers
2 1 (c), 2 (d), 3 (a), 4 (b)

35. Holiday plans

1 (a) B, D, F
  (b) if he runs out of money
  (c) many postcards
2 (a) two of: lots to see / excellent shopping / can practise English
  (b) one of: her cousin stayed with her / it's her turn (you won't
      get a mark for saying her aunt lives in America)
  (c) to see if she likes it or not / to get to know the country

36. Holiday problems

1 Sample translation:
  Holidays are fun, when everything goes to plan.
  Last summer my neighbours complained very much about
  their hotel. My parents never go abroad, because they don't
  speak the language and don't want to have an accident in a
  foreign country.
2 (a) gut, (b) laut, (c) voll, (d) gut, (e) schmutzig

37. Asking for help

1 (i) A, (ii) D, (iii) C, (iv) A, (v) B
2 (a) one of: on a tree / by a lake
  (b) the weather was especially lovely
  (c) one of: unable to stand/get up / in terrible pain

38. Transport

1 (a) one of: drove on / stopped
  (b) one of: wide / lovely
  (c) he didn't know
  (d) one of: given Emil a ticket / read his paper
  (e) nobody was interested in him ('he was small' will not
      get a mark)
2 B, E, F

39. Travel

1 Sample translations:
  (a) Mein Vater findet Autos praktisch.
  (b) Ich fahre lieber mit dem Bus.
  (c) Der Verkehr in meiner Stadt ist wirklich laut.
  (d) Letzte Woche sind wir auf der Autobahn gefahren.
  (e) Wir haben Karten gespielt, weil es Spaß macht / denn
      es macht Spaß.

2 Sample translation:
  Meine Mutter hatte gestern eine schreckliche Fahrt
  zum / ins Büro. Ihr Auto hatte eine Panne neben der Tankstelle.
  Sie muss jetzt mit dem Rad fahren, während das Auto in der
  Garage / Autowerkstatt ist. Ich wünsche mir, dass weniger Leute
  mit dem Auto fahren würden, weil die öffentlichen Verkehrsmittel
  hier so gut sind.

40. Directions

1 (a) Auto, (b) gute, (c) überqueren, (d) richtig, (e) Park
2 (i) C, (ii) A, (iii) D, (iv) C

41. Eating in a café

1 (a) young people
  (b) any one of: tasty / good value
  (c) no dogs
2 (a) food brought to you
  (b) choice not so good / annoying to have to order/pay first
  (c) doesn't do it every day
  (d) celebration / birthday

42. Eating in a restaurant

1 Student's own answer
2 1 (b), 2 (d), 3 (a), 4 (c)

43. Shopping for food

1 (a) Trauben, (b) Bananen, (c) Äpfel, (d) Pflaumen,
  (e) Trauben
2 (a) exhausted
  (b) had to buy the goods/fruit and veg first
  (c) getting on with customers
  (d) adding up
  (e) good weather / sunshine

44. Opinions about food

1 (a) Zucker
  (b) um die Zähne zu schützen / wegen der Zähne
  (c) one of: gelingt ihm nie / macht nicht gern Diät
  (d) gesund / gut
  (e) was sie isst / ihre Diät

45. Buying gifts

Sample answer:

SPEAKING TRACK 69

Listen to the recording

Teacher: Beschreib mir das Foto.
Student: Das Bild zeigt ein wunderbares
Geschäft, wo man schöne Andenken vom
Urlaub kaufen kann. Ich denke, dass die
Frau im Bild in diesem Geschäft arbeitet.
Sie trägt warme Kleidung, weil es wahrscheinlich
kalt ist. Sie lächelt und holt ein Souvenir vom Regal.
Vielleicht hat jemand das gerade gekauft und sie muss
es jetzt als Geschenk einpacken.
Teacher: Ich finde Geschenke wichtig. Was meinst du?
Student: Mir ist es wichtig, Geschenke zu geben, und ich weiß, dass
ich immer sehr gern Geschenke bekomme. Wenn ein Freund oder ein
Familienmitglied Geburtstag hat, sollte man ihm etwas geben.
Solche Geschäfte wie das im Foto sind meiner Meinung nach ideal
für ein Reisegeschenk, und ich würde wahrscheinlich hier viele
Geschenke kaufen.
Teacher: Hast du ein Geschenk bekommen, das dir nicht gefallen hat?
Erzähl mir davon.
Student: Als ich in der Grundschule war, haben meine Eltern mir zum
zehnten Geburtstag einen neuen Schreibtisch als Geschenk gegeben.
Ich war extrem enttäuscht, weil ich mir ein blaues Fahrrad gewünscht
hatte. Ich war schlecht gelaunt, weil das so ein schreckliches
Geschenk war. Jetzt kann ich darüber lachen, aber diesen Geburtstag
werde ich nie vergessen.
Teacher: Wirst du in Zukunft deine Geschenke im Geschäft oder im
Internet kaufen?
Student: In Zukunft werde ich meine Geschenke bestimmt im Internet
kaufen, weil die Auswahl so viel besser ist als in den
großen Geschäften. Das Internet ist praktischer, finde ich, weil

ich viele Ideen recherchieren und vergleichen kann, bevor ich das Geschenk dann bestellen muss. Natürlich muss man dann auf die Lieferung warten, aber das wäre nicht zu lange, denke ich.
Teacher: Findest du es wichtig, Dankesbriefe zu schreiben?
Student: Ich finde, Dankesbriefe sind ziemlich altmodisch, aber man sollte mindestens eine SMS schicken oder eine E-Mail schreiben, um sich für das Geschenk zu bedanken. Ich denke, dass es sehr großzügig ist, wenn zum Beispiel meine Tanten mir Geld zum Geburtstag schicken, und deswegen sende ich ihnen immer sofort eine Kurznachricht. Wenn ich mich nicht richtig bei ihnen bedanken würde, hätte ich Angst, dass sie mir nichts zum nächsten Geburtstag schicken würden!

46. Weather
1 (i) B, (ii) A, (iii) A, (iv) C, (v) D

47. Places to see
1 Part (a)
(i) B, (ii) A, (iii) D

Part (b)
(i) C, (ii) B, (iii) D

48. At the tourist office
1 (a) A, C, F
(b) one of: souvenir hunters / shoppers
(c) most museums closed Mondays
2 B, E, G

49. Describing a town
1 (i) C, (ii) D, (iii) A, (iv) B, (v) D

50. Describing a region
1 1 Teacher: Wo ist dein Wohnort?
Student: Ich wohne in einem Dorf im Nordwesten von England in der Nähe von Liverpool. Die nächste Stadt in der Gegend heißt St Helens und sie hat ungefähr hunderttausend Einwohner.

SPEAKING TRACK 70

Listen to the recording

2 Teacher: Was kann man in deiner Gegend machen?
Student: Hier im Dorf hat man viele Möglichkeiten: man kann im Park Fußball spielen oder nach St Helens fahren und ins Stadion gehen, um ein Rugbyspiel zu sehen. Hier in der Gegend kann man auch ins Kino oder Theater gehen, und in der Stadt gibt es viele Restaurants und Nachtlokale.

3 Teacher: Was hast du am Wochenende in deiner Gegend gemacht?
Student: Am Samstag bin ich zuerst mit dem Bus in die Stadt gefahren, um neue Sportschuhe zu kaufen. Danach habe ich meine Freunde im Café getroffen und wir sind anschließend zusammen zum Skatepark gefahren. Das hat Spaß gemacht, obwohl das Wetter sehr kalt war.

4 Teacher: Was würdest du einem Touristen in deiner Gegend empfehlen?
Student: Als Tourist hier muss man unbedingt das Glasmuseum in St Helens besuchen, weil das sehr interessant ist. Ich würde auch einen Besuch an der Küste empfehlen, weil die Landschaft dort sehr eindrucksvoll ist. Es wäre auch gut, an einem Abend einmal ins Theater zu gehen.

5 Teacher: Was möchtest du an deiner Gegend ändern?
Student: Ich würde einen Freizeitpark in dieser Gegend bauen, weil der uns hier im Moment fehlt. Junge Leute würden das super finden, besonders wenn man den Park einfach mit dem Bus von überall her erreichen könnte.

2 Student's own answers

51. Tourism
1 Sample translation:
My parents like going abroad. They like writing postcards. I never go to an airport, because I don't like flying. Last year I went by train to Switzerland. In the summer I am going on a coach / bus trip to the coast.
2 A, E, G

52. Countries
1 Sample translation:
If you visit a foreign country, you have to plan it in advance. You can go to a travel agency or you can research everything on the internet. But I also recommend a tourist guide as it is very useful. When I went to Turkey last year, I planned the journey and that was worth it.
2 (a) two of: Austrian / likes going abroad / goes on holiday with her family
(b) one of: learning Spanish at school / can order food in Spanish
(c) better climate
(d) has no coast/sea

Topic 3 School

53. School subjects
1 Sample translations:
(a) Ich finde Mathe schwierig / schwer.
(b) Ich mag Naturwissenschaften nicht. / Ich mache Naturwissenschaften nicht gern.
(c) Wir haben jeden Mittwoch Erdkunde / Geografie.
(d) Gestern habe ich eine gute Note in Chemie bekommen.
(e) Ich mag Kunst, weil es interessant ist.
2 Sample translation:
Dieses Jahr habe ich Italienisch und Französisch gewählt. In der Grundschule haben wir keine Fremdsprachen gelernt. Meine Klasse hat auch Spanisch und wir reisen / fahren bald nach Madrid. Ich würde sehr gern Latein lernen, weil das für die Universität nützlich ist.

54. Opinions about school
1 (i) D, (ii) C, (iii) A, (iv) B, (v) C
2 (a) one of: bullying / pupils didn't feel safe
(b) one of: disruptive pupils / pupils chatting/texting each other
(c) one of: needs good grades/education for career/future / to become a dentist

55. School day
1 (a) Nähe, (b) neun, (c) liebt, (d) unappetitlich, (e) gern
2 (i) B, (ii) A, (iii) D

56. Types of schools
1 (a) A, C, G
(b) one of: pressure / that she has to learn / she can't just do sport
(c) wants to become a vet so needs good grades / a good *Abitur*
2 (a) two of: pupils impolite / school day long / school day tiring
(b) being able to wear her own clothes
(c) one of: teachers / staff
(d) school finishing time

57. School facilities
1 Sample translation:
Today we have chemistry in the laboratory. I prefer sport in the gym / sports hall. Our school is great because the food in the canteen tastes good / is tasty. On Tuesday I drank a can of cola in the art room. That's not allowed!
2 A, D

58. School rules
1 1 (b), 2 (d), 3 (a), 4 (c)

59. Pressures at school
1 (i) B, (ii) B, (iii) D, (iv) C, (v) A

60. Primary school
1 (a) Liza, (b) Halina, (c) Jens, (d) Ömer, (e) Liza
2 (a) sing
(b) going to the park
(c) eating fruit
(d) swimming lesson

61. Success at school

1 **Part (a)**
   (i) 18
   (ii) (every) Friday
   (iii) a competition
   Part (b)
   (i) March
   (ii) one of: classroom / sports ground / laboratory

62. Class trips

1 **Sample translation:**
   Every class goes on a class trip once a year.
   Most trips take place in Germany, but some pupils also go abroad. I would like to go to America, but I know that is too expensive. Last year I was really looking forward to the week at the coast, but then I was ill on the day of travel.

2 A, C, G

63. School exchange

1 (a) Sophie, (b) Kevin, (c) Shiyan, (d) Anna, (e) Shiyan, (f) Sophie
2 (a) 2008
   (b) overcame language problems
   (c) one of: East European food / their own food / food specialities from home (you need to have the adjective 'East European' or something to indicate it is their own type of food to score a point here)
   (d) one of: got to know Germany / informed Germans about their home country
   (e) peace

64. School events

1 **Sample answer:**
   Teacher: Was für Events gibt es an deiner Schule?
   Student: Im Sommer findet immer ein großes Sportfest statt.
   Teacher: Wie findest du Schulevents?
   Student: Ich finde Schulevents toll, weil sie interessant und spannend sind.
   Teacher: Wie war das Event letztes Jahr?
   Student: Es hat viel Spaß gemacht und ich habe eine Medaille gewonnen.
   Teacher: Toll. Hast du eine Frage?
   Student: Was ist das nächste bei dir?
   Teacher: Nächstes Semester haben wir ein Musikfest. Hast du noch eine Frage?
   Student: Nimmst du gern an Events teil?
   Teacher: Ja, sehr gern.
2 Student's own answers

Topic 4 Future aspirations, study and work

65. Future study

1 (a) one of: to have best chance of getting high grade in the *Abitur* / it's the best in the area
   (b) one of: work experience at vet's / she became aware that she preferred to work with animals rather than people
   (c) one of: it's cheaper / to gain new experiences / to become independent
2 (a) Gymnasium, (b) lockerer, (c) Möglichkeiten, (d) manche, (e) Arbeit

66. Jobs

1 (a) there are so many options / an increasing number of choices
   (b) (any one) with animals / people
   (c) know it from books / everyday life OR so that people stop asking them unwanted questions.
2 A, C, G

67. Professions

1 **Sample translation:**
   My mother is a vet. She works in the centre of town. Her work pleases her / She likes her work, because she likes helping other people. Last week our dog had an accident. Tomorrow we are going to the park again for the first time.
2 A, C, D

68. Job wishes

1 (a) one of: prefer to do apprenticeship (you won't get a mark for saying they want to be mechanics / plumbers)
   (b) one of: to get a good job / earn a high salary
   (c) one of: there's a good selection / there are plenty
   (d) one of: doesn't matter what the weather is like / has air conditioning
   (e) one of: learn useful things for the world of work / impress employer

69. Opinions about jobs

1 (a) B, E, F
   (b) shift work
   (c) one of: wages / salary / pay
2 (a) standing by changing rooms
   (b) shouted at staff in front of customers
   (c) thirty days' annual leave / 10% discount in all departments
   (d) one of: promotion prospects / variety of work

70. Job adverts

1 (a) conditions, (b) cathedral, (c) experience, (d) proud, (e) collect
2 A, C, F

71. Applying for a job

1 Student's own answers
2 1 (c), 2 (a), 3 (d), 4 (b)

72. Job interview

1 Student's own answers
2 **Sample answer:**
   Teacher: Was für einen Job suchen Sie?
   Student: Ich suche einen Job als Babysitterin.
   Teacher: Wann wollen Sie arbeiten?
   Student: Ich will im Sommer arbeiten.
   Teacher: Wo arbeiten Sie im Moment?
   Student: Im Restaurant.
   Teacher: Warum sind Sie für diesen Job geeignet?
   Student: Ich arbeite gern mit Kindern und ich kann gut kochen.
   Teacher: Schön. Haben Sie eine Frage?
   Student: Wie viel verdiene ich als Babysitterin?
   Teacher: 12 Euro pro Stunde.

73. Languages beyond the classroom

1 (i) A, (ii) B, (iii) D, (iv) C, (v) B

74. Volunteering

1 **Sample translation:**
   Letzten Monat habe ich freiwillige Arbeit im Krankenhaus gemacht. Obwohl die Arbeit mir gefallen hat, habe ich die Tage sehr anstrengend gefunden. Dieses Jahr arbeitet mein Bruder als Freiwilliger in einem Tierheim. Er möchte sehr gern im Ausland arbeiten, um Tieren zu helfen, die unter Krankheiten leiden.
2 (a) einfach, (b) neu, (c) abwechslungsreich, (d) anstrengend, (e) anstrengend

75. Training
1 (a) Supermarkt, (b) Restaurant, (c) Büro, (d) Kaufhaus,
   (e) Büro
2 (a) a sales person
   (b) Saturday job
   (c) one of: give advice / help
   (d) one of: if there are exams / if has to take exams

76. Part-time jobs
1 (i) A, (ii) C, (iii) D, (iv) B, (v) A
2 B, D

77. CV
1 1 (D), 2 (A), 3 (E), 4 (C), 5 (B)

Topic 5 International and global dimensions

78. Global sports events
1 (a) Ich **bin** mit meinen Freunden bei einem Fußballspiel.
   Das Wetter **ist** sonnig und warm, und es **gibt** viel Lärm.
   Ich **finde** Sportevents sehr stressig, und ich **sehe** sie mir
   lieber im Fernsehen an.
   (b) Wir **sind** bei der Fußballmeisterschaft. Das **macht** mir Spaß,
   weil ich ein großer Fußballfan **bin**. Sportevents **finde** ich immer
   sehr spannend, aber diese Eintrittskarte **ist** wirklich zu teuer.
   (c) Wir **sehen** uns ein Fußballspiel an. Die Stimmung im Stadion
   ist wunderbar und die Fußballer **sind** sehr begabt. Ich **liebe**
   solche Events, weil die Sportler mich **inspirieren**.
2 Student's own answers

79. Global music events
1 Student's own answers
2 1 (c), 2 (d), 3 (b), 4 (a)

80. Being green
1 **Sample translations:**
   (a) Ich recycle immer Flaschen.
   (b) Ich fahre nie mit dem Rad.
   (c) Meine Eltern tragen immer Pullover im Haus.
   (d) Gestern hat meine Freundin Sara den Müll getrennt.
   (e) Sie hat geduscht, weil das umweltfreundlich ist.
2 (a) share/inform about their ideas on green living (you won't get
       a mark for saying they live an environmentally friendly life)
   (b) one of: no car / solar energy from roof
   (c) posts photos of rubbish left/environmental damage in woods
   (d) one of: writes own vegan recipes / gives make-up advice
   (e) one of: gives energy-saving tips / uploads videos to help

81. Protecting the environment
1 **Sample translation:**
   The air pollution in my town is dreadful, especially
   when the weather is very hot. The airport is only five
   kilometres away from our flat and the motorway is also
   very close. We should all protect the environment and use public
   transport more often rather than travelling / driving by car.
2 B, D, F

82. Natural resources
1 (i) A, (ii) D, (iii) C, (iv) B, (v) A

83. Campaigns
1 1 (b), 2 (e), 3 (d), 4 (a), 5 (c)
2 **Sample answer:**
   Teacher: Beschreib mir das Foto.
   Student: Das Bild zeigt zwei Teenager,
   die sehr glücklich aussehen. Sie lächeln und ich
   denke, sie arbeiten vielleicht freiwillig. Es gibt
   noch zwei Leute im Bild, und sie tragen alle die
   gleichen T-Shirts, weil sie zusammen arbeiten. Sie sind in einem
   Raum, wo es viele Kartons gibt mit Lebensmitteln, die man
   gesammelt hat. Hinten im Bild sieht man auch Kleidung.

Ich weiß nicht, was die zwei Leute machen, aber sie sortieren
vielleicht die Kleidung.
Teacher: Ich finde es wichtig, Spendenaktionen für andere
zu machen. Was meinst du?
Student: Mir ist es wichtig, Spendenaktionen für andere zu
machen, weil zum Beispiel viele Familien in Armut leben.
An unserer Schule haben wir oft Spendenaktionen und ich finde
das toll. Zum Beispiel sammeln wir Lebensmittel und Kleidung
für Menschen in unserer Stadt oder wir backen und verkaufen
Kuchen und Kekse in der Pause. Jede Klasse macht eine
Spendenaktion und dann geben wir alles einer Organisation.
Teacher: Wie hast du anderen geholfen?
Student: Letztes Jahr habe ich Lebensmittel für andere Leute
in unserer Stadt gespendet, weil mir das sehr am Herzen liegt.
Unsere Klasse hat außerdem während des ganzen Jahres viele
Aktionen organisiert, um Geld für Organisationen in der Gegend
zu sammeln, die Lebensmittel retten. Das Beste war aber der
Spendenlauf im Park. Ich habe extra dafür im Sportverein
trainiert, und am Tag des Spendenlaufs war ich superfit. Ich bin
die zehn Kilometer extrem schnell gelaufen und danach konnte
ich Geld von Verwandten und Freunden für diese
Organisationen sammeln.
Teacher: Wie, meinst du, kann man am besten anderen helfen?
Student: Tja, das ist eine gute Frage. Der Spendenlauf hat mir
besonders gut gefallen, aber manche Schüler sind nicht so sportlich,
und ich denke, sie nehmen lieber an einem Konzert oder einem
Event teil. Man kann auch helfen, wenn man freiwillige Arbeit
macht oder babysittet. Statt Geld zu sammeln, kann man auch
Lebensmittel oder Kleidung für eine Organisation sammeln.
Teacher: Wie ist deine Meinung zum Tierschutz?
Student: Ich bin totaler Tierfan, also denke ich, dass der
Tierschutz sehr wichtig ist. In Zukunft möchte ich freiwillig
in einem Tierheim arbeiten. Idealerweise hilft man aber auch
anderen Menschen. Wenn ich etwas spenden wollte, würde ich
gern für Tiere oder für andere Leute spenden.

84. Good causes
1 (a) Schule, (b) Gebäck, (c) online, (d) Keine,
   (e) Ideen
2 B, D, F

Grammar

85. Gender and plurals
1 (a) der Abfalleimer
   (b) das Kino
   (c) die Krankenschwester
   (d) der Rucksack
   (e) das Handy
   (f) das Restaurant
   (g) die Autobahn
   (h) der Sportlehrer
   (i) die Umwelt
2 (a) Das Haus ist modern.
   (b) Der Schüler heißt Max.
   (c) Die Schülerin heißt Demet.
   (d) Der Computer ist kaputt.
   (e) Der Zug fährt langsam.
   (f) Die Bank ist geschlossen.
   (g) Die Zeitung kostet 1 Euro.
   (h) Das Buch ist langweilig.
3 (a) Wir haben die Pizza gegessen.
   (b) Wir können das Krankenhaus sehen.
   (c) Ich mache die Hausaufgabe.
   (d) Vati kauft den Pullover.
   (e) Liest du das Buch?
   (f) Ich wasche den Wagen.

4 Haus S, Buch S, Männer P, Autos P, Häuser P, Supermarkt S,
Tisch S, Mann S, Supermärkte P, Tische P, Handys P, Zimmer E,
Bilder P, Computer E

86. Cases and prepositions

1 (a) um die Ecke
(b) durch die Stadt
(c) ohne ein Auto
(d) für die Schule
(e) für einen Freund
(f) gegen die Wand
(g) durch einen Wald
(h) die Straße entlang

2 (a) mit dem Bus
(b) seit dem Sommer
(c) zu der Bank / zur Bank
(d) nach der Party
(e) bei einem Freund
(f) von einem Onkel
(g) gegenüber der Tankstelle
(h) außer der Lehrerin
(i) aus dem Raum

3 (a) wegen des Wetters
(b) während der Stunde
(c) trotz des Regens

87. Dative and accusative prepositions

1 (a) Wir fahren in die Stadt.
(b) Meine Schwester ist in der Schule.
(c) Das Essen steht auf dem Tisch.
(d) Ich steige auf die Mauer.
(e) Wir hängen das Bild an die Wand.
(f) Jetzt ist das Bild an der Wand.
(g) Die Katze läuft hinter einen Schrank.
(h) Wo ist die Katze jetzt? Hinter dem Schrank.
(i) Die Bäckerei steht zwischen einem Supermarkt und einer Post.
(j) Das Flugzeug fliegt über die / der Stadt.
(k) Ich stelle die Flaschen in den Schrank.
(l) Der Bus steht an der Haltestelle.

2 (a) Die Kinder streiten sich über das Fernsehprogramm.
The children are arguing about the TV programme.
(b) Wir freuen uns auf das Fest.
We are looking forward to the festival / celebration.
(c) Ich ärgere mich oft über die Arbeit.
I often get cross about work.
(d) Martin hat sich an die Sonne gewöhnt.
Martin has got used to the sun.
(e) Wie lange warten Sie auf die Straßenbahn?
How long have you been waiting for the tram?

3 (a) auf dem Land – *in the country*
(b) vor allem – *above all*
(c) auf die Nerven – *on (someone's) nerves*
(d) auf der rechten Seite – *on the right*
(e) im Internet – *on the internet*

88. *Dieser / jeder, kein / mein*

1 (a) *this man* – dieser Mann
(b) *with this man* – mit diesem Mann
(c) *this woman* – diese Frau
(d) *for this woman* – für diese Frau
(e) *that animal* – jenes Tier
(f) *on that animal* – auf jenem Tier

2 (a) Unsere Schwester heißt Monika.
(b) Ich habe keinen Bruder.
(c) Meine Schule ist nicht sehr groß.
(d) Hast du deinen Laptop vergessen?
(e) Wie ist Ihr Name, bitte? *(No ending necessary)*
(f) Meine Lehrerin hat ihre Schulbücher nicht mit.
(g) Wo steht Ihr Auto? *(No ending necessary)*
(h) Wir arbeiten in unserem Büro.

(i) Wo ist eure Wohnung? *(Note spelling change)*
(j) Meine Lieblingsfächer sind Mathe und Informatik.
(k) Wie heißt deine Freundin?
(l) Leider haben wir keine Zeit.
(m) Ihre E-Mail war nicht sehr höflich.
(n) Olaf geht mit seinem Freund spazieren.
(o) Adele singt ihre besten Hits.
(p) Wo habt ihr euer Auto stehen lassen? *(No ending necessary)*
(q) Ich habe keine Ahnung.
(r) Ich habe keine Lust.
(s) Das war mein Fehler.
(t) Meiner Meinung nach …

89. Adjective endings

1 (a) Die intelligente Schülerin bekommt gute Noten.
(b) Wir fahren mit dem nächsten Bus in die Stadt.
(c) Hast du den gelben Vogel gesehen?
(d) Der altmodische Lehrer ist streng.
(e) Ich kaufe dieses schwarze Kleid.
(f) Die neugebauten Reihenhäuser sind schön.
(g) Heute gehen wir in den modernen Freizeitpark.
(h) Wir müssen dieses schmutzige Fahrrad sauber machen.
(i) Morgen gehen wir ins neue Einkaufszentrum.
(j) Der verspätete Zug kommt um 1 Uhr an.

2 (a) München ist eine umweltfreundliche Stadt.
(b) Ich suche ein preiswertes T-Shirt.
(c) Marta hat ihre modische Handtasche verloren.
(d) Wir haben unsere schwierigen Hausaufgaben nicht gemacht.
(e) Ich habe ein bequemes Bett gekauft.
(f) Das ist ein großes Problem.
(g) Das war vielleicht eine langweilige Stunde!
(h) Diese idiotischen Leute haben das Spiel verdorben.
(i) Mein Vater hat einen schweren Unfall gehabt.
(j) Klaus liebt seine neue Freundin.
(k) Wir haben kein frisches Obst.
(l) Maria hat einen grünen Mantel gekauft.

90. Comparisons

1 (a) Mathe ist langweilig, Physik ist langweiliger, aber das langweiligste Fach ist Kunst.
(b) Oliver läuft schnell, Ali läuft schneller, aber Tim läuft am schnellsten.
(c) Berlin ist schön, Paris ist schöner, aber Wien ist die schönste Stadt.
(d) Rihanna ist cool, Katy Perry ist cooler, aber Taylor Swift ist die coolste Sängerin.
(e) Metallica ist lauter als Motörhead.
(f) Bremen ist kleiner als Hamburg.
(g) Deine Noten sind schlecht, aber meine sind noch schlechter.
(h) Ich finde Englisch einfacher als Französisch, aber Deutsch finde ich am einfachsten.
(i) Skifahren ist schwieriger als Radfahren.
(j) Mein Auto ist billiger als dein Auto, aber das Auto meines Vaters ist am billigsten.

2 (a) Ich bin jünger als du.
I am younger than you.
(b) Die Alpen sind höher als der Snowdon.
The Alps are higher than Snowdon.
(c) München ist größer als Bonn.
Munich is bigger than Bonn.
(d) Meine Haare sind lang, Timos Haare sind länger, aber deine Haare sind am längsten.
My hair is long, Timo's hair is longer, but your hair is the longest.
(e) Fußball ist gut, Handball ist besser, aber Tennis ist das beste Spiel.
Football is good, handball is better, but tennis is the best game.

3 (a) Ich spiele gern Basketball.
(b) Ich esse lieber Gemüse als Fleisch.
(c) Am liebsten gehe ich schwimmen.

91. Personal pronouns

1 (a) Ich liebe dich.
   (b) Liebst du mich?
   (c) Kommst du mit mir?
   (d) Mein Bruder ist nett. Ich mag ihn gern.
   (e) Ich habe keine Kreditkarte. Ich habe sie verloren.
   (f) Ein Geschenk für uns? Danke!
   (g) Wir haben euch gestern gesehen.
   (h) Haben Sie gut geschlafen?
   (i) Die Party ist bei mir.
   (j) Rolf hatte Hunger. Ich bin mit ihm essen gegangen.
   (k) Vergiss mich nicht!
   (l) Wie heißt du?
   (m) Wie heißen Sie?
   (n) Meine Schwester ist krank. Gestern sind wir zu ihr gegangen.

2 (a) Schwimmen fällt mir schwer.
   (b) Mmmm, Eis! Schmeckt es dir?
   (c) Aua! Das tut mir weh!
   (d) Leider geht es uns nicht gut.
   (e) Wer gewinnt im Fußball? Das ist mir egal.
   (f) Es tut uns leid.

92. Word order

1 (a) Um 6 Uhr beginnt die Fernsehsendung.
   (b) Jeden Tag fahre ich mit dem Bus zur Arbeit.
   (c) Leider sind meine Eltern krank.
   (d) Hier darf man nicht rauchen.

2 (a) Gestern haben wir Eis gegessen.
   (b) Manchmal ist Timo ins Kino gegangen.
   (c) Letztes Jahr ist Ali nach Frankreich gefahren.
   (d) Heute Morgen hast du Pommes gekauft.

3 (a) Ich fahre jeden Tag mit dem Rad zur Schule.
   (b) Gehst du am Wochenende mit mir zum Schwimmbad?
   (c) Wir sehen oft im Wohnzimmer fern.
   (d) Mehmet spielt abends Tischtennis im Jugendclub.
   (e) Mein Vater arbeitet seit 20 Jahren fleißig im Büro.
   (f) Willst du heute Abend mit mir im Restaurant Pizza essen?

93. Conjunctions

1 (a) Claudia will Sportlehrerin werden, weil sie sportlich ist.
   (b) Ich kann dich nicht anrufen, weil mein Handy nicht funktioniert.
   (c) Wir fahren nach Spanien, weil das Wetter dort so schön ist.
   (d) Du darfst nicht im Garten spielen, weil es noch regnet.
   (e) Peter hat seine Hausaufgaben nicht gemacht, weil er faul ist.
   (f) Ich mag Computerspiele, weil sie so aufregend sind.

2 (a) Du kannst abwaschen, während ich koche.
   (b) Wir kaufen oft ein, wenn wir in der Stadt sind.
   (c) Ich kann nicht zur Party kommen, da ich arbeiten werde.
   (d) Lasst uns früh aufstehen, damit wir wandern können.
   (e) Meine Eltern waren böse, obwohl ich nicht spät nach Hause gekommen bin.
   (f) Ich habe es nicht gewusst, dass du krank bist.
   (g) Papa hat geraucht, als er jung war.
   (h) Ich weiß nicht, wie man einen Computer repariert.
   (i) Wir können schwimmen gehen, wenn das Wetter gut ist.
   (j) Wir müssen warten, bis es nicht mehr regnet.

94. More on word order

1 (a) Wir fahren in die Stadt, um Lebensmittel zu kaufen.
   (b) Viele Leute spielen Tennis, um fit zu werden.
   (c) Boris spart Geld, um ein Motorrad zu kaufen.
   (d) Meine Schwester geht zur Abendschule, um Französisch zu lernen.
   (e) Ich bin gestern zum Imbiss gegangen, um Pommes zu essen.

2 (a) Das Orchester beginnt zu spielen.
   (b) Wir hoffen, Spanisch zu lernen.
   (c) Oliver versucht, Gitarre zu spielen.

3 (a) das Mädchen, das Tennis spielt
   (b) der Junge, der gut singt

   (c) der Mann, der Deutsch spricht
   (d) das Haus, das alt ist
   (e) das Fach, das schwer ist
   (f) das Auto, das kaputt ist
   (g) die Tasse, die voll ist

95. The present tense

1 (a) wir gehen   (b) er findet
   (c) sie singt   (d) ich spiele
   (e) ihr macht   (f) du sagst
   (g) es kommt   (h) sie schwimmen
   (i) ich höre   (j) wir trinken

2 (a) Was liest du?
       What are you reading?
   (b) Schläfst du?
       Are you asleep?
   (c) Annabelle isst nicht gern Fleisch.
       Annabelle doesn't like eating meat.
   (d) Kerstin spricht gut Englisch.
       Kerstin speaks English well.
   (e) Nimmst du Zucker?
       Do you take sugar?
   (f) Ben fährt bald nach Berlin.
       Ben is going to Berlin soon.
   (g) Hilfst du mir, bitte?
       Will you help me please?
   (h) Mein Onkel gibt mir 20 Euro.
       My uncle is giving me 20 euros.

3 er spricht, du siehst, sie fährt, er liest

96. Separable and reflexive verbs

1 (a) Wir kommen bald an.
   (b) Er fährt um 7 Uhr ab.
   (c) Wir laden oft Filme herunter.
   (d) Wie oft siehst du fern?
   (e) Wo steigt man aus?
   (f) Ich mache die Tür zu.

2 (a) Wir sind bald angekommen.
   (b) Er ist um 7 Uhr abgefahren.
   (c) Wir haben oft Filme heruntergeladen.
   (d) Wie oft hast du ferngesehen?
   (e) Wo ist man ausgestiegen?
   (f) Ich habe die Tür zugemacht.

3 (a) Ich interessiere mich für Geschichte.
       I am interested in history.
   (b) Sara freut sich auf die Ferien.
       Sara is looking forward to the holidays.
   (c) Erinnerst du dich an mich?
       Do you remember me?
   (d) Wir langweilen uns in der Schule.
       We get bored at school.
   (e) Ich habe mich noch nicht entschieden.
       I haven't decided yet.
   (f) Tina hat sich heute nicht geschminkt.
       Tina hasn't put on make-up today.
   (g) Habt ihr euch gut amüsiert?
       Have you enjoyed yourselves?
   (h) Unser Haus befindet sich in der Nähe vom Bahnhof.
       Our house is situated near the train station.

97. Commands

1 (a) Parken Sie hier nicht!
   (b) Sprechen Sie nicht so laut!
   (c) Steigen Sie hier aus!
   (d) Fahren Sie nicht so schnell!
   (e) Kommen Sie herein!
   (f) Gehen Sie geradeaus!
   (g) Kommen Sie bald wieder!
   (h) Geben Sie mir 10 Euro!

2 (a) Steh auf!
  (b) Schreib bald!
  (c) Komm her!
  (d) Nimm zwei!
  (e) Bring mir den Ball!
  (f) Hör auf!
  (g) Benimm dich!
  (h) Setz dich!

98. Present tense modals
1 (a) Ich kann nicht schnell laufen.
  (b) Wir müssen bald Kaffee kaufen.
  (c) Kinder sollten keinen Alkohol trinken.
  (d) Claudia mag nicht schwimmen.
  (e) Schüler dürfen hier nicht sitzen.
  (f) Wir wollen Pommes essen.
  (g) Hier darf man parken.
  (h) Meine Eltern wollen eine neue Wohnung mieten.
  (i) Du kannst gut Fußball spielen.
  (j) Sie sollten höflich sein.
2 (a) Im Kino darf man nicht rauchen.
  (b) Wir möchten zur Bowlingbahn gehen.
  (c) Meine Freunde wollen zu Hause bleiben.
  (d) Ihr müsst weniger essen.
  (e) Man soll nicht viel Zucker essen.
  (f) Ergül kann gut Gitarre spielen.
  (g) Kannst du mir bei meinen Hausaufgaben helfen?
  (h) Man darf hier nie spielen.
  (i) Wir müssen mit der Straßenbahn fahren.
  (j) Ich will meinen Salat nicht essen.

99. Imperfect modals
1 (a) ich wollte   (b) wir mussten
  (c) sie konnten   (d) sie durfte
  (e) man sollte   (f) er mochte
  (g) wir wollten   (h) Jutta konnte
2 (a) Du solltest gesund essen.
  (b) Wir mussten nach Hause gehen.
  (c) Ella mochte nicht Musik hören.
  (d) Wir wollten im Internet surfen.
  (e) Ich konnte gut Tischtennis spielen.
  (f) Ihr durftet spät ins Bett gehen.
3 (a) Möchten Sie Tennis spielen?
  (b) Wir könnten einkaufen gehen.
  (c) Ich möchte ein Eis essen.
  (d) Könntest du mir helfen?

100. The perfect tense 1
1 (a) Wir haben Minigolf gespielt.
  (b) Habt ihr neue Schuhe gekauft?
  (c) Hast du deine Oma besucht?
  (d) Was hat er gesagt?
  (e) Ich habe Spanisch gelernt.
  (f) Hast du diese Zeitung gelesen?
  (g) Dennis hat mir ein Geschenk gegeben.
  (h) Wir haben einen tollen Film gesehen.
2 (a) Wohin bist du gefahren?
  (b) Wir sind nach Mallorca gefahren.
  (c) Ich bin zu Hause geblieben.
  (d) Usain Bolt ist schnell gelaufen.
  (e) Meine Mutter ist nach Amerika geflogen.
  (f) Der Zug ist abgefahren.
3 (a) Abdul hat 12 Stunden geschlafen.
  (b) Wir haben unsere Hausaufgaben gemacht.
  (c) Wohin bist du gefahren?
  (d) Ich bin spät nach Hause gekommen.
  (e) Habt ihr Britta gesehen?

101. The perfect tense 2
1 (a) geschwommen   (b) gewesen
  (c) geschlossen   (d) gegessen

  (e) gestanden   (f) gesessen
  (g) geschrieben   (h) gestorben
  (i) gesprochen   (j) getroffen
  (k) geworden   (l) getrunken
  (m) genommen   (n) gesungen
  (o) gehabt
2 (a) Wir haben eine E-Mail geschrieben.
  (b) Wir haben uns um 6 Uhr getroffen.
  (c) Niemand ist gestorben.
  (d) Hast du mein Handy genommen?
  (e) Ich habe eine Bratwurst gegessen.
  (f) Er hat ein Glas Cola getrunken.
  (g) Wir sind im Meer geschwommen.
  (h) Marita hat Italienisch gesprochen.
3 (a) vergessen   (b) angekommen
  (c) empfohlen   (d) verloren
  (e) besucht   (f) heruntergeladen
  (g) abgefahren   (h) ausgestiegen

102. The imperfect tense
1 (a) Ich spielte am Computer.
  (b) Was sagtest du?
  (c) Nina kaufte Chips.
  (d) Die Schüler lernten Englisch.
  (e) Es schneite im Winter.
  (f) Peter lachte laut.
2 (a) Es war gestern kalt.
  (b) Wir hatten auf der Party viel Spaß.
  (c) Paul war im Krankenhaus.
  (d) Meine Eltern hatten drei Kinder.
  (e) Ich war gestern im Imbiss.
  (f) Hattest du Angst?
3 (a) Es gab viel zu essen. I
  (b) Wir sitzen im Kino. P
  (c) Es tut mir leid! P
  (d) Ich fahre nach Berlin. P
  (e) Er kommt früh an. P
  (f) Er saß im Wohnzimmer. I
  (g) Sie kamen um 6 Uhr an. I
  (h) Wie findest du das? P
  (i) Aua! Das tat weh! I
  (j) Ich fand es gut. I
  (k) Es gibt nicht viel zu tun. P
  (l) Klaus fuhr zu schnell. I

103. The future tense
1 (a) Susi geht nächstes Jahr auf die Uni.
  (b) Wir fahren im Sommer nach Ibiza.
  (c) Er kommt übermorgen zu uns.
  (d) Ich bleibe heute Abend zu Hause.
  (e) Bringst du am Wochenende deine Schwester mit?
2 (a) Ich werde um 6 Uhr abfahren.
  (b) Wirst du am Wochenende Musik hören?
  (c) Werdet ihr Pizza essen?
  (d) Wir werden die Prüfung bestehen.
  (e) Nächstes Jahr werden wir nach Afrika reisen.
  (f) Daniel wird einen Film herunterladen.
  (g) Ich werde ein Problem mit meinem Laptop haben.
  (h) Bayern München wird das Spiel gewinnen.
  (i) Meine Freunde werden um 9 Uhr ankommen.
  (j) Meine Schwester wird im August heiraten.
3 Student's own answers.

104. The conditional
1 (a) Wenn wir Zeit hätten, würden wir einkaufen gehen.
  (b) Wenn meine Eltern Geld hätten, würden sie ein Auto kaufen.
  (c) Wenn ich Kinder hätte, würde ich sie lieben.
  (d) Wenn Tanja nicht krank wäre, würde sie Skateboard fahren.
  (e) Wenn du fleißiger wärst, würdest du deine Prüfung bestehen.
  (f) Wenn das Wetter besser wäre, würden wir Sport treiben.

2 (a) Wenn ich Krankenschwester wäre, würde ich mich freuen.
  (b) Wenn er Klempner wäre, würde er viel verdienen.
  (c) Wenn wir in einer Fabrik arbeiten würden, wären wir müde.
  (d) Wenn wir Glasflaschen hätten, würden wir sie recyceln.
  (e) Wenn ich Hunger hätte, würde ich eine Bratwurst essen.
  (f) Wenn Manya und Timo Talent hätten, würden sie in einer Band spielen.
3 Student's own answers.
4 Student's own answers.

105. The pluperfect tense
1 (a) Wir hatten Kaffee und Kuchen bestellt.
  (b) Hattest du Spaß gehabt?
  (c) Ich hatte eine neue Stelle bekommen.
  (d) Wir hatten unsere Freunde eingeladen.
  (e) Als ich nach Hause gekommen war, habe ich gegessen.
  (f) Kagan war zur Bäckerei gegangen.
  (g) Sie waren zu Hause geblieben.
  (h) Ich war mit dem Auto nach Frankfurt gefahren.
2 (a) Es war nicht passiert.
  (b) Ich hatte dir eine E-Mail geschickt.
  (c) Hattest du dich nicht geschminkt?
  (d) Ich war sehr früh eingeschlafen.
  (e) Opa war noch nie nach London gefahren.
  (f) Warst du zur Haltestelle gegangen?
  (g) Wir hatten unseren Müll zur Mülldeponie gebracht.
  (h) Er hatte zwei Computerspiele heruntergeladen.
  (i) Die Fabrik war sehr laut gewesen.
  (j) Fatima hatte Abitur gemacht.

106. Questions
1 (a) Spielt Kevin oft am Computer?
  (b) Hast du dein Handy verloren?
  (c) Wollen wir Volleyball spielen?
  (d) Studiert Hakan Informatik?
  (e) Geht ihr morgen zum Sportzentrum?
2 (a) Bist du zum Supermarkt gefahren?
  (b) Wird Ayse Chemie studieren?
  (c) Ist dein Auto kaputt?
  (d) Isst du gern Bratwurst mit Pommes?
  (e) Wird es morgen regnen?
3 *who?* – wer? *what?* – was? *how?* – wie? *when?* – wann? *why?* – warum? *where?* – wo? *how many?* – wie viele? *what kind of?* – was für? *whose?* – wessen? *who with?* – mit wem?
4 Student's own answers.

107. Time markers
1 (a) gestern – *past*
  (b) früher – *past*
  (c) bald – *future*
  (d) letzte Woche – *past*
  (e) heute – *present*
  (f) normalerweise – *present*
  (g) vor 2 Wochen – *past*
  (h) morgen – *future*
  (i) nächste Woche – *future*
  (j) jetzt – *present*
2 1 C
  2 E
  3 A
  4 F
  5 B
  6 D
3 (a) Nächste Woche werde ich mein Betriebspraktikum machen.
  (b) Heute Abend sieht Ulli fern.
  (c) In Zukunft wird man Strom sparen.
  (d) Bald wirst du einen Unfall haben.
  (e) Manchmal treffen wir uns mit unseren Freunden.
  (f) Neulich war ich bei meinem Onkel.

  (g) Vorgestern hat Metin sein Betriebspraktikum begonnen.
  (h) Jeden Tag gehe ich zur Bäckerei.

108. Numbers
1 (a) 421
  (b) 1644
  (c) 68
  (d) 301
  (e) 97
  (f) 105
  (g) 17
  (h) 653
2 (a) Es ist **zwanzig** nach **neun**. (20, 9)
  (b) Ausverkauf! **Fünfzehn** Prozent Rabatt! (15)
  (c) Es ist **dreizehn** Grad. (13)
  (d) Ich habe **sechshundertfünfzig** Euro gewonnen. (650)
  (e) Der Zug kommt um **zwölf** Minuten vor **sieben** an. (12, 7)
  (f) Es gibt **dreißig** Schüler in meiner Klasse. (30)
3 (a) 12.3.   (b) 13.7.   (c) 28.12.
  (d) 1.4.   (e) 3.1.   (f) 17.6.
4 (a) Mein Geburtstag ist am ersten November.
  (b) Saschas Geburtstag ist am siebten September.
  (c) Das Konzert findet am zwölften Mai statt.
  (d) Die Ferien beginnen am zweiten Juli.

Tests

109. Test: Listening 1
1 (i) C, (ii) A, (iii) D
2 A, C, E

110. Test: Listening 2
1 B, D, G
2 (a) Ausland, (b) gleichen, (c) zuverlässig, (d) Viertel, (e) überrascht

111. Test: Listening 3
1 (a) one of: so quiet in class he wasn't noticed / never wanted to answer a question
  (b) one of: she likes him now / happy to go to school with him / no longer avoids him
  (c) two of: cheeky, talkative / got detentions / rarely did homework / had to go to the Head
  (d) has a nicer new group of friends
2 B, D, G

112. Test: Speaking 1
1 Sample answer:
Teacher: An welchem Tag fahren Sie und wohin?
Student: Am Montag will ich nach Berlin fahren.
Teacher: Warum fahren Sie dorthin?
Student: Ich besuche meine Großmutter, denn sie hat Geburtstag.
Teacher: Um wie viel Uhr wollen Sie abfahren?
Student: Um halb zehn, bitte.
Teacher: Was für eine Fahrkarte wollen Sie?
Student: Hin und zurück, bitte.
Teacher: Sehr gut. Haben Sie eine Frage?
Student: Wieviel kostet die Fahrkarte, bitte?
Teacher: 45 Euro.

SPEAKING TRACK 74

Listen to the recording

2 Sample answer:
Teacher: Was machst du gern online?
Student: Ich chatte gern mit Freunden und sehe meine Lieblingsserien im Internet.
Teacher: Wie findest du Computerspiele und warum?
Student: Ich finde sie fantastisch, weil sie unterhaltsam sind.

SPEAKING TRACK 75

Listen to the recording

Teacher: Was hast du letztes Wochenende online gemacht?
Student: Ich habe Videos heruntergeladen.
Teacher: Interessant. Hast du eine Frage?
Student: Wie oft benutzt du einen Computer?
Teacher: Jeden Tag. Hast du noch eine Frage?
Student: Was machen wir nach dem Abendessen am Computer?
Teacher: Wir hören Musik.

113. Test: Speaking 2

1 Sample answer:

Teacher: Beschreib mir das Foto.
Student: Dieses Foto ist interessant, finde ich. Die vier Leute interessieren sich sehr für den Umweltschutz, denke ich. Sie sammeln hier Abfall, um diese Gegend zu verbessern. Vielleicht finden sie alte Dosen und Plastiktüten, die Leute hier weggeworfen haben.

Teacher: Wie findest du Umweltschutz?
Student: Ich versuche umweltfreundlich zu sein und ich trenne gern den Müll zu Hause. Im Winter spare ich Energie, weil ich die Heizung nie hoch stelle. Ich ziehe lieber einen warmen Pullover an. Am liebsten fahre ich mit dem Rad in die Stadt, weil ich das Autofahren schrecklich finde.

Teacher: Wie warst du letzte Woche umweltfreundlich?
Student: Letzte Woche habe ich mich jeden Tag geduscht. So habe ich Wasser gespart. Ich habe meine alten T-Shirts zum Container gebracht, um sie zu recyceln. Ich bin überall mit dem Rad gefahren.

Teacher: Wie wirst du in Zukunft umweltfreundlicher sein?
Student: Ich werde nächsten Monat an der Fahrradwoche an der Schule teilnehmen. Zu Hause werde ich einen Nistkasten für Vögel bauen, und das wird interessant sein. Hoffentlich besuchen dann viele Vögelarten den Garten.

Teacher: Was ist für dich das größte Problem unseres Planeten?
Student: Für mich ist das das Aussterben von Tieren. Ich liebe alle Tiere und in Zukunft würde ich gern Tierarzt werden. Wir müssen alle Tierarten schützen. Für mich ist das schockierend, und meiner Meinung nach müssen wir etwas dagegen machen. Meinen Sie das auch?

2 Sample answer:

Teacher: Beschreib mir das Foto.
Student: Dieses Foto ist interessant und ich stelle mir vor, man hat es in der Nähe einer Großstadt gemacht. Die vier Leute interessieren sich sehr für den Umweltschutz und machen sich Sorgen über unseren Planeten. Deshalb sammeln sie hier Abfall, um diese Gegend zu verbessern. Die machen das, obwohl das Wetter kalt und windig ist. Vielleicht finden sie alte Dosen und Plastiktüten, die faule Besucher nicht mit nach Hause genommen haben.

Teacher: Ist dir Umweltschutz wichtig?
Student: Also, ich bin ziemlich umweltfreundlich, und so wie andere auch, trenne ich den Müll in der Schule und zu Hause, aber sonst mache ich nicht so viel, muss ich sagen. Ich finde es gut, dass man an der Kasse für Plastiktüten bezahlen muss, aber ich fahre immer noch lieber mit dem Auto als mit dem Rad.

Teacher: Wie warst du letzte Woche umweltfreundlich?
Student: Gute Frage! Also, zuerst habe ich geduscht, das ist viel umweltfreundlicher als zu baden, finde ich. Ich war aber ein bisschen zu spät aufgestanden, also musste meine Mutter mich mit dem Auto zur Schule fahren. An der Schule sind wir immer umweltfreundlich – wir müssen den Müll trennen, die Lichter ausschalten und Energie sparen.

Teacher: Wie könntest du also umweltfreundlicher werden?
Student: Da könnte ich noch vieles machen! Vielleicht könnte ich nächsten Monat an der Fahrradwoche an unserer Schule teilnehmen. Zu Hause möchte ich gern einen Nistkasten für

Vögel bauen, aber ich bin kein begabter Tischler/keine begabte Tischlerin, also werde ich das vielleicht nie machen!
Unprepared question:
Teacher: Was ist für dich das größte Problem unseres Planeten?
Student: Also für mich ist das ohne Zweifel das Aussterben von Tieren. Ich liebe Tiere aller Art und in Zukunft möchte ich Tierarzt werden. Wir müssen alle Tierarten schützen. Wussten Sie, dass es nur noch vier weiße Nashörner in der ganzen Welt gibt? Für mich ist das schockierend, und meiner Meinung nach müssen wir etwas dagegen machen.

114. Test: Reading 1

1 (a) Halina, (b) Frank, (c) Lena, (d) Yusuf, (e) Halina, (f) Yusuf

2 Sample translation:

My mother always saves energy. At home we all wear warm jumpers. That is annoying, because I prefer to wear T-shirts. Last Wednesday I didn't separate / sort the rubbish. Next week I will do that every day.

115. Test: Reading 2

1 (a) they want to lead a healthy life
(b) one of: they have sports clubs/school sports clubs / sports clubs used not to exist
(c) it will create an active country

2 (i) D, (ii) C, (iii) B, (iv) A, (v) C

116. Test: Reading 3

1 (a) his name also starts with the same three letters
(b) one of: noisily / burst in / ran in
(c) thinks he is on the run
(d) one of: face pales / eyes grow bigger
(e) stealing from a shop till

117. Test: Reading 4

1 (a) Halbbruder, (b) Schwester, (c) Vater, (d) Stiefmutter, (e) Schwester

2 Sample translation:

My father is a doctor in the country(side). He often has to work nights and then he comes home exhausted. He would much rather have another position / job where the hours are shorter.
He used to have a part-time job in a shop in the town centre, which he really enjoyed / liked.

118. Test: Writing 1

1 Sample answer:

Ich verbringe eine Woche Urlaub auf einem Campingplatz in Österreich. Ich schlafe gern im Zelt, aber morgens wache ich sehr früh auf, weil es hell ist.

2 Sample answer:

Hallo Sura,
meine Schule befindet sich zwei Kilometer von der Stadtmitte entfernt. Es ist eine gut ausgestattete Schule und wir haben eine große Aula. In der Pause kann man etwas in der Kantine kaufen oder auf dem Schulhof spielen. Nächste Woche gibt es ein Musikfest, wo alle Schüler an Konzerten teilnehmen.

3 Sample translations:

(a) Ich esse gern Pommes (Frites).
(b) Mein Bruder isst nie Fleisch.
(c) Meine Lieblingsnachspeise ist Kuchen mit Schokoladensoße.
(d) Am Wochenende habe ich eine große Flasche Cola getrunken.
(e) Am Abend war ich krank, und wir sind zum Krankenhaus gegangen / gefahren.

4 Sample translation:

Letztes Ostern haben meine Eltern viele Eier im Garten versteckt. Jedes Mal, wenn ich ein Ei gefunden habe, hat mein Bruder es sofort genommen. Nächstes Jahr werde ich keine Schokolade suchen, weil sie sehr ungesund ist. Ich würde das Geld lieber für Kleider ausgeben, die viel nützlicher sind.

120. Test: Writing 2

1 Sample answer:

Hallo Sadi,

ich wohne seit drei Jahren in einer großen Wohnung im dritten Stock eines modernen Hochhauses. Letztes Wochenende habe ich viele Stunden in meinem Schlafzimmer an der Konsole verbracht, weil das Wetter so schlecht war. In den Sommerferien gehe ich oft in den Sportverein, um Fußball mit Freunden dort zu spielen. Ich finde das gesünder als immer drinnen zu bleiben. Du musst mich bald besuchen, weil die Gegend hier echt schön ist. Wir können zusammen ins Freibad gehen oder eine Radtour machen. Das macht mir immer Spaß!

Dein(e) …

2 Sample answer:

Ein gesponserter Marathonlauf für ein Wasserprojekt in Afrika!

Nächsten Monat nehme ich an einem Marathonlauf in der Stadt teil, um Geld für ein wichtiges Wasserprojekt in Westafrika zu sammeln. Das ursprüngliche Wasserprojekt befindet sich in einem kleinen Dorf, wo die Frauen und Kinder früher zehn Kilometer zum Wasserholen gehen mussten. Mithilfe des Wasserprojektes fließt seit drei Jahren frisches Trinkwasser direkt in ihr Dorf hinein. Ich möchte jetzt ein ähnliches Wasserprojekt für ein anderes Dorf in der Gegend organisieren, und dafür bitte ich euch jetzt um eine Spende. Letztes Jahr habe ich viel Geld hier in der Schule für dieses Projekt gesammelt, indem ich Kuchen gebacken habe oder auch an gesponserten Aktivitäten teilgenommen habe. Dieses Jahr ist es mein Ziel, am Marathonlauf teilzunehmen, und es würde mich sehr freuen, wenn alle Schüler mir zu diesem Zweck etwas spenden könnten. Am Tag des Laufes werde ich ein bunt gestreiftes T-Shirt tragen, und ich könnte das Logo unserer Schule klar und groß darauf drucken. Es wäre toll, wenn ihr mir Geld spenden würdet.

Published by Pearson Education Limited, 80 Strand, London, WC2R 0RL.

www.pearsonschoolsandfecolleges.co.uk

Copies of official specifications for all Pearson qualifications may be found on the website: qualifications.pearson.com

Text, audio and illustrations © Pearson Education Limited 2017, 2021
Typeset and illustrations by Kamae Design, Oxford, and Newgen Knowledgeworks
Produced by Cambridge Publishing Management Ltd and Newgen Publishing UK
Cover illustration © Kamae Design Ltd

The right of Harriette Lanzer to be identified as author of this work has been asserted by her in accordance with the Copyright, Designs and Patents Act 1988.

First published 2021

24 23
10 9 8 7 6 5 4 3

British Library Cataloguing in Publication Data
A catalogue record for this book is available from the British Library

ISBN 978 1 292 41226 9

Printed by CPI Group (UK) Ltd, Croydon CR0 4YY

Acknowledgements
The author and publisher would like to thank the following individuals and organisations for permission to reproduce photographs:

(Key: b-bottom; c-centre; l-left; r-right; t-top)
Alamy Stock Photo: MBI/Stockbroker 17t, Sabine Lubenow 45tr; **Getty Images:** DisobeyArt/iStock 78t, AleksandarGeorgiev/E+ 113t, Prostock-Studio/iStock 118t; **Pearson Education Ltd:** Studio 8 8t, Jon Barlow 47br; **Shutterstock:** Dragana Gordic 83t.

Cover: Pearson Education Limited 2020

All other images © Pearson Education

We are grateful to the following for permission to reproduce copyright material:

Text
Page 10: excerpt from Ulrich Plenzdorf, *Die neuen Leiden des jungen W.* © Suhrkamp Verlag Frankfurt am Main 1976. All rights reserved by and controlled through Suhrkamp Verlag Berlin; **Page 12:** extract from *Die verlorene Ehre der Katharina Blum* by Heinrich Böll in *Heinrich Böll, Cologne Edition, Volume 18. 1971–1974*, edited by Viktor Böll and Ralf Schnell in collaboration with Klaus-Peter Bernhard © 2003 Kiepenheuer & Witsch GmbH & Co. KG, Cologne/Germany; **Page 27:** extract from *Pelle zieht aus und andere Weihnachtsgeschichten* (German edition) by Astrid Lindgren, Verlag Friedrich Oetinger GmbH, 2013 © The Astrid Lindgren Company and Verlag Friedrich Oetinger; **Page 38:** extract from Erich Kästner, *Emil und die Detektive* (1935) © Atrium Verlag AG, Zürich 2021; **Page 46:** extract from *Der Weltenwanderer: Zu Fuß um die halbe Welt* by Gregor Sieböck, p.132 (2010 4e), Verlagsanstalt Tyrolia Gesellschaft m.b.H; **Page 59:** extract from *Der Tag, an dem ich cool wurde* (German edition) by Juma Kliebenstein, Verlag Friedrich Oetinger GmbH 2010, pp.11–12, ISBN 978-3789140457; **Page 82:** *Nackt schlafen ist bio: Eine Öko-Zynikerin findet ihr Grünes Gewissen und die große Liebe* by Vanessa Farquharson, translated by Gerlinde Schermer-Rauwolf and Robert A. Weiß © Bastei Lübbe AG, Köln 2011; **Page 116:** extract from *Die unendliche Geschichte* by Michael Ende, Thienemanns (K.) Verlag pp.7–8, ISBN 978-3522176842, © 1979 Thienemann in der Thienemann-Esslinger Verlag GmbH, Stuttgart.

Notes from the publisher

1. While the publishers have made every attempt to ensure that advice on the qualification and its assessment is accurate, the official specification and associated assessment guidance materials are the only authoritative source of information and should always be referred to for definitive guidance.

Pearson examiners have not contributed to any sections in this resource relevant to examination papers for which they have responsibility.

2. Pearson has robust editorial processes, including answer and fact checks, to ensure the accuracy of the content in this publication, and every effort is made to ensure this publication is free of errors. We are, however, only human, and occasionally errors do occur. Pearson is not liable for any misunderstandings that arise as a result of errors in this publication, but it is our priority to ensure that the content is accurate. If you spot an error, please do contact us at resourcescorrections@pearson.com so we can make sure it is corrected.